RANDOM TABLES
DUNGEONS AND LAIRS

RANDOM TABLES
DUNGEONS AND LAIRS

The Game Master's Companion for Creating
Secret Entrances, Rumors, Prisons, and More

Dr. Timm Woods

ULYSSES PRESS

Published by:
ULYSSES PRESS
PO Box 3440
Berkeley, CA 94703
www.ulyssespress.com

ISBN: 978-1-64604-351-4
Library of Congress Control Number: 2022932317

Printed in the United States by Versa Press
10 9 8 7 6 5 4 3 2 1

Acquisitions editor: Casie Vogel
Managing editor: Claire Chun
Project editor: Tyanni Niles
Editor: Renee Rutledge
Proofreader: Anne Healey
Cover and interior design: what!design @ whatweb.com
Production: Winnie Liu
Artwork: cover—dungeon Midnight Coffee Design/shutterstock.com, dice kericanfly/shutterstock
  .com; interior—shutterstock.com

To my students, who teach me every day.

Contents

Doors & Barriers 109

Acknowledgments 128

About the Author 128

Introduction

Inky darkness stretches before you—those with darkvision see a pathway leading far into the depths of the earth. The stone of the archway above you is etched with ancient and unintelligible runes. Warm wind—like a deep, monstrous breath—wafts forth, and the sound of distant clanking can be heard. You are likely to be eaten by a monster. Beware, foolish mortal ...

... and WELCOME to the DUNGEON!

Your adventure has only just begun! This book is your key to the dungeons, crypts, and other ancient sites that fill the worlds of tabletop role-playing games (TTRPG) like Dungeons & Dragons. Every dungeon needs explorers and adventurers to delve into its depths, slay the monsters, and grab the loot. But behind every great dungeon is a great Game Master (GM), the designer and mastermind of the whole experience. It's up to the Game Master to decide what is around every corner, behind every door, and guarding every chest of treasure.

If you've ever been a Game Master, then you know it takes hard work and creativity. Tabletop role-playing games are fun to play, and running them as the Game Master and storyteller can be even more rewarding! But running these games can come with a lot of hats to wear—and that's before you even start to talk about creating unique locations and challenges to fill your game world! Dungeon crawls in particular can sometimes feel boring or repetitive if they aren't regularly injected with new elements or inspiration. Especially for newer GMs, designing your own dungeons can be a complicated and intimidating prospect.

One solution is reading established published adventures and studying famous dungeons from the past—both real and fantastic. These can give amazing ideas and exciting inspiration for how to create your own dungeons. But what if you had all those ideas at your fingertips?

This book of random tables gives you access to the best ideas that dungeons have to offer, all in one place. It's hard to imagine every possibility that could occur to adventurers exploring vast and intricate underground complexes—and now you don't have to! If you are searching for inspiration and new ideas, or simply trying to break away from the usual elements of your dungeon designs, then look no further than this book!

Random Dungeons

Inserting randomly generated content can be one of the most fun ways to approach Game Mastering. Random dungeons can be an excellent way to learn about how to Game Master, experience and explore the full catalog of dungeon possibilities, and find out what sort of dungeon elements you and your players like to run and play.

Generating dungeons with random dice rolls creates chaos, which can be a welcome delight in any adventure. It helps both experienced Game Masters and their veteran players break out of ruts, even the ones you might not notice. If you've never tried it before, it can be a fun experiment to run a whole session of dungeon crawling on the fly, improvising by randomly generating the content as you go. Experienced players will often be entertained just by knowing that the Game Master plans to use random content! Telling them the idea ahead of time allows players to get in on the fun, anticipating that whatever might be around the next corner will be just as surprising to the Game Master as it is to them.

Of course, it may be that you need a dungeon, and you need it now. It can happen to the best of Game Masters! Maybe you are pressed for time and didn't get the chance to plan; the players are here, it's game time, and you don't have an adventure ready. Maybe you did plan a particular idea for the session, but the players are uninterested or are just looking for a classic dungeon crawl instead. There's nothing wrong with giving the players what they want, and with this book, you always have a dungeon up your sleeve!

Or, it could be that you have time to plan, but you want inspiration. Dungeons can risk feeling like cookie-cutter clones without distinctive and unique details to set them apart. The tables in this book are filled with all manner of ideas that you may not yet have explored in the dungeons you've designed for your adventuring parties. You don't need to imagine everything yourself! This book will help shake things up at your table and lead players to new and unexpected themes, encounters, and other surprises.

How to Use This Book

To use this book, you will need your trusty dice sets on hand. When you wish to use one of the tables, roll the appropriate die indicated by the table, be it a d4, d6, d8, d10, d12, d20, or d100; then, find the result that corresponds to the number you rolled. Some tables will ask you to apply a modifier to the roll according to certain details about your dungeon. Those details will need to be established before rolling.

Let one roll inform the next in an unfolding story. Sometimes results that seem contradictory are interesting opportunities, but other times an incompatible result (such as an ice door in a lava-filled room) simply doesn't make sense and can be re-rolled or reinterpreted. You can stretch your imagination to make some surprising ideas work together; for example, if a dungeon built by a flying race has a surprising quantity of pits, this might indicate that they felt threatened by nearby land-dwellers. A villain whose bedroom randomly contains a statue of their greatest fear might seem silly but makes for a juicy narrative, and finding the story that the results generate for you can often be half the fun!

Often when you are building a dungeon, you may have some details that are already established, such as the location of the dungeon or the villain who inhabits it. Feel free to choose some details and roll others. This often makes for the most interesting dungeons! These tables will serve you well when filling in the blanks in a dungeon that might already be 10, 50, or 90 percent complete. Jump around and use the tables where they seem necessary; start and stop generating content as you see fit.

Even if you don't have so much as the seed of an idea for your dungeon or if you're generating one now in the middle of your game, you can still use these tables to generate an entire dungeon from scratch. To do so, follow these instructions:

First, you need the basic details, found in part 1, "Dungeon Essentials." The tables there will help you generate the core dungeon type (page 14), current status (page 16), and location (page 31) of the dungeon, as well as its original builders (page 27) and any rumors (page 19) surrounding it. These details will be the basis to anchor all of the rest of the dungeon.

Once the essentials are locked in, a great place to start is at the entrance to your dungeon, working your way inward. Generate the dungeon facade (page 48) as well as any secret entrances (page 55) or entrance defenses (page 52) that might come into play.

Details like lighting (page 35), temperature (page 37), air quality (page 38), water sources (page 41), food sources (page 42), noises (page 44), and odors (page 47) can be generated for the dungeon in its entirety and can serve as some of its defining characteristics. You can then move on to part 2, "Rooms & Halls," to procedurally generate the rooms (page 57) and connections (page 97) of your dungeon, generating additional details for each dungeon space as you move through the sub-tables. Or, you could start with the rooms and connections, then afterward outfit each space (or certain parts of the dungeon) with unique lighting, temperature, or noises to help distinguish them as the party moves through their expedition.

Finally, part 3, "Doors & Barriers," offers a variety of doors (page 110), locks (page 121), and other sealing methods to impede parties trying to make their way through your dungeon. It is recommended that you place these wherever the dungeon builders or current inhabitants would value security or privacy. Sprinkle them liberally around areas with a high concentration of enemies or treasure.

And there you have it—a fully detailed dungeon space for your questing heroes to conquer. Let your imagination be the torch that lights the way. Good luck, and good gaming!

Dungeon Essentials

Dungeon Types (d10)

Each dungeon is a unique adventuring prospect, a one-of-a-kind location that was likely built for a specific purpose. As such, it can be difficult to neatly classify the diverse array of dungeons that might populate your campaign—but there are some rough categories. Roll on this table to generate a dungeon type in which you can set your next adventure. Your dungeon type will be used again for future rolls in this book.

Type	Description
1: Barrow	Located below the surface of a cairn, mound, hill, or mountain, this dungeon with primarily earthen ruins is where ancient rulers and warriors would be laid to rest.
2: Fortress	With fortified walls and defenses, this dungeon is designed to allow an armed population to live, guard, and secure the location against other armies.
3: Home	This dungeon serves as the domestic home for a particular individual or villain, reflecting the personality of the owner.
4: Lair	This dungeon serves as the base or headquarters for a particular villain, group, or force, reflecting the aesthetics and culture of the occupants.
5: Maze	A winding, complex network of tunnels and passages is designed to confuse, challenge, or kill those who would try to reach the end of this dungeon.
6: Mine	The inhabitants of this dungeon work (or previously worked) in its rough, winding tunnels and unfinished portions to mine ore and other resources from the earth.
7: Prison	With complex and inhospitable tunnels, this dungeon is designed to contain prisoners, a particular kind of prisoner, or one prisoner in particular, keeping them securely locked away from the rest of the world.
8: Temple	With accommodations for the worship of certain gods, deities, or other entities, this dungeon likely reflects the general or unique aesthetic of the entity in question.
9: Tomb	A particularly important individual, or a large population, has been laid to rest in the crypts and graves of this dungeon, which is distinguished by primarily stone ruins.
10: Vault	Designed to contain valuables, a particular kind of valuable, or one treasure in particular, this dungeon keeps its contents warded, guarded, and secured.

Current Status (d12)

Any dungeon worthy of an adventure has probably acquired a rich and colorful history since its construction. It may have traded hands, suffered the effects of time, or been converted for a new purpose depending on whether the original builders are still around to maintain it. The residents of the surrounding region might not know the dungeon's status, and adventurers may need to seek it out or hope for the best. Roll on this table to generate the current status and condition of your dungeon.

Status	Description
1: Ascendant	Not only is this dungeon intact and inhabited, it is also thriving and growing in size, population, and influence. The rising power of the dungeon makes it a threat and keeps would-be heroes from venturing closer.
2: Destroyed	This dungeon has been absolutely wiped off the map by some major cataclysm. Somehow, against all odds, portions of the original structure have survived and may still be explored.
3: Fortified	This dungeon has been occupied and fortified either by its original inhabitants or by new occupants. More individuals may be living in the dungeon than was intended by the original builders, and additional defenses may have been added to protect the fortifying forces.
4: Long Lost	This dungeon has disappeared from records and common knowledge, or at least its location has. Even knowledge about how to find this locale would be valuable to the right interested parties.
5: Natural Space	This dungeon is a natural area consisting of a geological formation. It was not fashioned with conscious intention, but has now been outfitted with a purpose by its current occupants.
6: Occupied by Original Builders	This dungeon is still occupied by its original builders (see page 27), though it may have traded hands with other factions in the past. These builders constructed the dungeon for a particular purpose and likely still seek to complete that objective.
7: Partly Conquered	This dungeon has been partly conquered by an army or powerful faction that has a large quantity (if not high quality) of soldiers to aid in their conquest. They are likely hostile to the party, but also to other, older inhabitants of the dungeon.

Status	Description
8: Partly Explored	This dungeon has been partly surveyed, looted, or otherwise explored by another faction besides the party. It may be a rival adventuring group or guild, or some other good or evil faction. This may make the dungeon more or less dangerous.
9: Rebuilt	This dungeon fell into ruin long ago, and locals likely assume it to be still abandoned. However, recently it has undergone rebuilding and renovation efforts, which may have been carried out secretly. The rebuilders might be the original dungeon inhabitants or new occupants who believe themselves to be carrying on their legacy.
10: Ruined	This dungeon has fallen into ruin, and large portions of it are collapsed or otherwise damaged. It is likely unable to fulfill its originally intended function but can perhaps still serve a portion of that purpose for its current occupants.
11: Sealed	This dungeon has been permanently sealed to prevent access by outside intruders, or perhaps to seal away something even more terrible. There may be other, unknown ways into and out of the dungeon, or perhaps the seals have weakened or can be overcome by the right individual, magic, or key.
12: Supposedly Abandoned	This dungeon was abandoned by its original occupants sometime in the more recent past, but by now may have drawn the attention of other occupants. Few have any reason to venture toward it, making it a convenient and likely lair for new inhabitants and creatures.

Rumors (d100)

Dungeons are often mysterious locations, and many become the center of at least one rumor about their nature, origins, or what lies beyond their entrance. The rumor may or may not be true and is more likely than not a misinterpreted or partially understood truth. Rumors of a dungeon of sufficient age may have faded into the legends and ancient myths of the surrounding region. Roll on this table to generate one or more unique rumors about your dungeon.

Rumor	Description
1–3: Armed Presence	This dungeon is rumored to house an army of unknown (but likely surprisingly large) size that has been growing there for years with the intention of being unleashed upon the surrounding region soon. The army will likely disperse if their leader, objective, or strength is somehow compromised.
4–6: Bandit Presence	Rumor has it that this dungeon is home to inhabitants who rob and steal from the locals of the nearby regions and those who travel through their territory. This behavior has drawn the attention of many locals and other outside forces who are unhappy with the impact the bandits have had on their way of life.
7–8: Beset by Treachery	Treacherous individuals are said to hide within the ranks of this dungeon's inhabitants. The inhabitants themselves likely know about the problem, or it is a secret only known among outsiders to the dungeon. These traitors may feed information to the party or otherwise aid them on their adventure, if the party comes prepared to work with them.
9–10: Cult Rituals	A church, magical group, or cult may be using this dungeon as the site of their rituals—either for its convenience or because its specific function, nature, and/or location have proven conducive to their magic.
11: Dark Trade	This dungeon is rumored to be the source of a particular kind of illegal, distasteful, or monstrous resource that is being traded with local criminals and black marketeers. This resource or at least maintaining its trade, is likely useful to the dungeon inhabitants, as well as other criminal and noncriminal outside factions.
12–14: Deadly Presence	A predator, magical energy, or monstrous force has a reputation for causing the death of locals and possibly even daring adventurers who have ventured close to this dungeon. Signs of these deaths have confirmed the dungeon as the source of the presence, but perhaps not its true nature.

Rumor	Description
15: Divine Presence	A deity or other godlike being likely resides in a special chamber or at the heart of this dungeon's structure. The being might be a demigod, a newborn or dying god, a newly created god, or a mortal transitioning into a god, but even a weakened god is still capable of immense power and likely has an influence over the nearby region.
16: Draconic Presence	This dungeon is rumored to be the home or lair of a particularly famous or powerful dragon. The dragon may be ancient and legendary; most locals believe it to be dead, but whether or not it still lives in some form is unclear.
17–18: Enemy Presence	Individuals or forces who have somehow garnered the personal enmity of particular powerful, well-connected, or authoritative figures in the local region are believed to have taken residence here. The rewards offered to adventurers willing to explore the dungeon are notably higher than would be expected and can likely be negotiated even higher. However, it may not be clear who the real villain is: the one in the dungeon, or the one condemning them as an enemy.
19: Ghostly Presence	A particularly famous or powerful ghost is said to haunt this dungeon. Their presence likely manifests in particular locations at particular times outside of the dungeon, but it is clear that the dungeon is the source of the haunting, as well as whatever unfinished business may plague them.

Rumor	Description
20: Great Library	This dungeon is rumored to contain a large collection of ancient, valuable, and perhaps even lost books and tomes. The rumors hint at any quirks the collection of books may possess.
21-22: Great Loot	Fortune-hunters and treasure-seekers are drawn to a large quantity of a particular kind of loot that this dungeon is said to contain. Rumors may hint at any quirks the treasure may possess.
23: Great Lore	A particular secret or piece of lore associated with this dungeon attracts the attention of scholars and mystics. The rumors may hint at any prices or dangers associated with learning the lore.
24-25: Great Magic	This dungeon is rumored to contain either a magical construct or apparatus, or the remains of a great ritual or spellcasting wrought here at an earlier time in history. This magic has probably caused sustained supernatural effects around and throughout the area of the dungeon.
26: Great Prison	Rumors speak of a vast prison with many different types of prisoners in this dungeon. The rumors likely discuss the quality and conditions of the prison, as well as any particular quirks it may have (see page 94).
27-29: Great Prize	A particularly impressive prize associated with this dungeon attracts the attention of fortune-hunters and treasure-seekers. The rumors may hint at any quirks the treasure may possess.
30-31: Great Treasure	The prospect of myriad prizes and loot attracts the attention of fortune-hunters and treasure-seekers to this dungeon. Rumors hint at any quirks the treasure may possess.
32-33: Haunting Presence	An eerie and mysterious supernatural presence, likely of one or more ghosts, or some other kind of undead (or else something posing as one), is said to roam this dungeon. Stories about this place are likely muddled by the fear it instills, and few are willing to get close enough to see, hear, or feel a glimpse of the presence and learn a hint of its true nature.
34: Hints of Accidents	A history of accidents, or of one major accident, follows this dungeon. It may have been an experiment gone wrong, a magical cataclysm, or the result of an attack, but the accident left a mark on the dungeon and a vivid memory amongst the locals.
35-36: Hints of Construction	A large-scale or otherwise significant construction project is taking place within this dungeon. Rumors hint at something as simple as an expansion, or at a project of vast resources or monumental magic whose implications might extend far beyond the dungeon's borders.

Rumor	Description
37: Hints of Experiments	Telltale signs throughout the local region in the form of pollution, chemical exhaust or runoff, magical corruption, or escaped experimental victims give vague hints as to the nature of the experiments taking place within the dungeon.
38: Illusory Presence	A powerful illusory force may account for some, or all, of this dungeon's external appearance. The dungeon may be designed to look ruined when it is actually intact or intact when it is actually ruined. The illusion may conceal dungeon defenses or make defenders appear where there are none.
39: Local Entrance	This dungeon is rumored to have a local point of entry within the very village, town, or city where the party hears the rumor. The entry is likely secret (see page 55). If a local entry to the dungeon would be impossible or implausible, this may be a magical entrance, or a person or key capable of granting entry or passage.
40: Magical Restrictions	Forces within this dungeon are said to limit what magic spellcasters can use within. Summoning and teleportation magic, as well as other spells, may be restricted in their effectiveness and usefulness while within or near the dungeon.
41–42: Mercenary Presence	A faction, army, or group of individuals who are selling their services throughout the region have drawn attention to this dungeon, which is rumored to be their headquarters. The mercenaries' true objectives—most likely, but not necessarily as combatants—are the primary cause for speculation.
43–44: Murderous Presence	This dungeon is rumored to be the source of premeditated murders throughout the region. The dungeon inhabitants have likely used stealth and subterfuge to ambush, assassinate, poison, or otherwise eliminate enemies of their cause.
45–46: Natural Disaster	The destructive forces of nature, in the form of a recent or long-ago earthquake, flood, volcanic eruption, or other natural disaster, have scarred this dungeon.
47–49: New Evidence	Recently discovered evidence in or around this dungeon suggests that locals and historians have been mistaken about a key detail concerning its origins, purpose, or the events that have taken place within it. The new evidence may make the dungeon seem more or less ominous; either way, interest in exploring the location has been renewed.

Rumor	Description
50–52: Newly Discovered	This dungeon is rumored to have been newly discovered, either for the first time since its construction or after a long period of being lost. A lucky coincidence, human curiosity, natural movement of the earth, or something more magical may have led to the discovery
53: Portal Presence	An active portal to another world is said to operate within this dungeon, likely at the heart of the structure. This portal allows access to and from this other world, and likely causes secondary leaks and disruptions in the planar boundaries surrounding the dungeon.
54–57: Predatory Presence	A group of monstrous creatures, or one great monstrous creature, whose predations are noticed throughout the region, have taken refuge within this dungeon. Locals may see the predator(s) out hunting, or more likely they have found tracks, corpses, and other signs of their hunting or foraging in the area.
58–60: Prisoner Presence	This dungeon is rumored to contain a particular prisoner or prisoners whose lives and freedom mean a great deal to one or more locals in the region. Rescuing these prisoners and getting them back to civilization will be no easy task, depending on the individual prisoner and their condition.

Rumor	Description
61-63: Resource Presence	A particular kind of magical or mundane resource that is likely valuable, precious, or even unique in the local region is said to be housed within this dungeon. This resource, or at least possession of it, is likely useful to the dungeon inhabitants, as well as a great many other outside factions.
64-65: Saboteur Presence	This dungeon is rumored to be home to inhabitants who sabotaged the work and/or trade of the locals of the nearby regions, likely for the purpose of discouraging their proximity to the dungeon. This behavior has drawn the attention of many locals and other outside forces who are unhappy with the impact of the saboteurs on their way of life.
66-68: Secret Entrances	One or more secret means of entry (see page 55), of which even the dungeon inhabitants may be ignorant, lend access to this dungeon. This secret entrance could certainly be used by the party to bypass some of the dungeon's defenses.
69: Sinking Foundations	Fighting a losing battle with its own structural integrity, this dungeon's unsteady foundations or shifting geological circumstances have caused it to begin slowly but steadily sinking into its environment. While the process is slow, its effects will be noticed and even felt by the adventurers during their expedition.
70: Source of Atonement	This dungeon is rumored to contain the opportunity for a holy warrior, mystic, or other servants of the gods or forces of goodness to redeem themselves. The redemption may be the result of a source of holy cleansing power within the dungeon, or due to the presence of a great evil to be purged by the supplicant.
71-72: Source of Evidence	Evidence of a crime or event that would either incriminate or absolve an accused local can be found here. Finding the evidence may be more complicated than simply exploring the dungeon, and returning with the evidence intact and presentable is another challenge altogether.
73-75: Source of a Theft	This dungeon is rumored to be the source of a recent successful theft (or "adventure" as some might call it) of a particularly valuable item or prize. The successful heist hints at the stolen treasure, the treasure that still might await future explorers, and the dangers that the thief or thieves overcame to acquire their loot. It is possible that someone will come looking for the lost treasure.

Rumor	Description
76–78: Supernatural Phenomena	Unusual or supernatural phenomena in the local region can be sourced to this dungeon. The phenomena may be miraculous or malign, ranging from the dead returning to life to frogs raining down from the sky. While public opinion may vary, the phenomena have certainly grabbed everyone's attention.
79–80: Threats Forthcoming	Whispers, heralds, or even dark omens or words written in the sky threaten the local region from the direction of this dungeon. The threats may be general, or may single out a specific individual, family, or faction.
81: Toll-Taker Presence	Inhabitants of this dungeon exact tolls and taxes upon those who travel through their territory. This behavior has drawn the attention of locals, who are likely unhappy about the impact the tolls have on their prosperity and travel options.
82–84: Torn by Conflict	Two or more factions within the dungeon are vying for control of the population, territory, resources, or other sources of magical or mundane power within the dungeon. The conflict may be brewing, or it may have erupted into full civil war already.
85–87: Undead Presence	A particular kind of undead, or one particularly powerful undead monster, plagues or haunts this dungeon. The undead likely leaves telltale signs of its presence through its hunting, passage, or mere existence.

Rumor	Description
88–90: Unearthed Evil	Miners or builders dug too greedily and too deep within this dungeon, accidentally releasing some ancient evil that had been dormant for generations. Rumors of the unearthed evil may have reached town, but not details as to the unearthed entity's identity.
91–92: Unusual Fauna	A particular kind of animal populates this dungeon and its surrounding region. The animal may be supernatural or dangerous, or may simply be a unique mundane species; either way, it likely has unique properties that make it useful or dangerous to locals.
93–94: Unusual Flora	A particular kind of plant life surrounds this dungeon and its vicinity. This vegetation may be supernatural, dangerous, or simply a unique mundane species; either way, it likely has unique properties that make it useful or dangerous to locals.
95–96: Unusual Trade	A particular kind of magical or mundane resource that is likely valuable, precious, or even unique in the local region is traded here. Dungeon inhabitants, as well as a great many other outside factions, likely benefit from this trade.
97–98: Unusual Weather	Stemming from this dungeon, unusual or supernatural weather patterns in the local region, or even across the wider world, are drawing the attention of many. The dungeon's location is likely the epicenter and strongest point of these weather conditions, which may serve as a useful defensive measure.
99–100: Wizard Presence	This dungeon is rumored to be the tomb or active lair of a particularly famous or powerful wizard. The wizard may be ancient and legendary; most locals believe them to be dead, but whether or not they still live in some form is unclear.

Original Builders (d100)

In many cases, the current occupants of a dungeon are not the same individuals who oversaw its original construction. These former occupants might be long gone; nonetheless, their mark is clear in the architecture, layout, ancient traps, and other features of the dungeon. Depending on the age of the dungeon, several waves of occupants may have come and gone over the years. Roll on this table to generate a distinctive group or force to be the original builders of your dungeon.

1: Ancient Dragons

2: Ancient Evil Ruler

3: Ancient Good Ruler

4: Ancient Just Ruler

5: Ancient Mad Ruler

6: Ancient Otherworldly Predecessors

7: Ancient Powerful Ruler

8: Ancient Primordial Beings

9: Ancient Weak Ruler

10: Ancient Wizards

11: Aquatic Peoples

12: Bandits

13: Barbarian Tribe

14: Benevolent Fey Folk

15: Benevolent Undead

16: Bird People

17: Celestials

18: Centaurs

19: Cyclopes

20: Dark Elves

21: Dark Fey Folk

22: Dark Priesthood

23: Death Cultists

24: Draconic Disciples

25: Draconic Peoples

26: Dragons

27: Druidic Circle

28: Druidic Disciples

29: Duergar Dwarves

30: Dwarven Craftsmen

31: Dwarven Lord

32: Dwarven Miners

33: Eldritch Aberrations

34: Eldritch Cultists

35: Elemental Beings

36: Elemental Cultists

37: Elemental Disciples

38: Elemental Peoples

39: Elven Craftsfolk

40: Elven Lord

41: Elven Wizards

42: Evil Archmage

43: Evil Cultists

44: Evil Gods/Godlike Beings

45: Evil Knightly Order

46: Evil Lich

47: Evil Lich (Disembodied)

48: Evil Wizards

49: Fiendish Cultists

50: Fiends

51: Fishfolk

52: Frogfolk

53: Genius Craftspeople

54: Genius Craftsperson

55: Giants

56: Gnolls

57: Gnomes

58: Goblinoids

59: Good Gods/Godlike Beings

60: Halflings

61: Harpies

62: Insectoid Peoples

63: Knightly Order

64: Kobolds

65: Lizardfolk

66: Local Evil Ruler

67: Local Good Ruler

68: Local Just Ruler

69: Local Mad Ruler

70: Local Weak Ruler

71: Local Wizards

72: Lost Peoples

73: Machine People

74: Mad Archmage

75: Medusas/Gorgons

76: Merfolk

77: Miners

78: Minotaurs

79: Monks

80: Mummy Lord

81: Naga

82: Noble Wizards

83: Ogres

84: Orcs

85: Plant People

86: Priestly Order

87: Ranger Lodge

88: Religious Disciples

89: Sentient Animals

90: Serpent People

91: Shadow People

92: Shapeshifters

93: Titans

94: Treefolk

95: Vampire

96: Warrior Order

97: Winged People

98: Wizard School

99: Wood Elves

100: Yetis

Location (d100)

The journey to reach the doorstep of a dungeon is often a difficult quest in its own right. The most remote dungeons are also correspondingly the most mysterious and unexplored, and likewise filled with the greatest and most unfamiliar dangers and treasures. Remote dungeons limit the party's ability to rest and resupply, forcing them to plan for the expedition thoughtfully—or pay the price. Roll on this table to generate an exciting and interesting location for your dungeon.

1: Amidst a Coral Reef

2: Amidst a Field of Barrows

3: Amidst Remote Hills

4: Atop a Frozen Mountain Peak

5: Atop a High Plateau

6: Atop a High and Narrow Spire

7: Atop a Huge Hill

8: Atop a Mountain Peak

9: Beneath a Castle

10: Beneath a Cemetery

11: Beneath a Holy Site

12: Beneath a Home or Estate

13: Beneath a Major City

14: Beneath a Massive Rock

15: Beneath a Modest Town

16: Beneath a Remote Village

17: Beneath a Ruined Tower

18: Beneath a Small Hamlet

19: Beside a Lava Rift

20: Beside a Remote Lake

21: Beside an Old Road

22: Bottom of a Lake

23: Bottom of a Massive Sinkhole

24: Bottom of a Vast Chasm

25: Bottom of the Ocean

26: Cursed Demon-Infested Lands

27: Deep Beneath a Desert

28: Deep Beneath a Mountain

29: Deep in a Corrupted Deadland

30: Deep in a Corrupted Forest

31: Deep in a Desert

32: Deep in a Dry Desert Badland

33: Deep in a Felled Forest

34: Deep in a Forbidden Marsh

35: Deep in a Forbidden Sacred Glade

36: Deep in a Frozen Wasteland

37: Deep in a Glacial Rift

38: Deep in a Haunted Forest

39: Deep in a Jungle

40: Deep in a Remote Wetland

41: Deep in a Ruined Wasteland

42: Deep in a Sacred Land

43: Deep in a Scorched Forest

44: Deep in a Swamp

45: Deep in an Ancient Forest

46: Deep in an Arctic Tundra

47: Deep in Bandit Territory

48: Deep in the Plains

49: Deep Underground

50: Edge of a Forest Cliff

51: Edge of a Huge Ravine

52: Edge of a Sea-Cliff

53: Edge of the Swamp

54: Floating in the Sky (Roll again to see above what.)

55: Halfway Up a Canyon Wall

56: Halfway Up a Cave-Riddled Hillside

57: Halfway Up a Cliff

58: Halfway Up the Walls of a Quarry

59: Heart of a Crater

60: Heart of a Garden Maze

61: Heart of a Growth of Giant Plants

62: Heart of a Mountain

63: Heart of a Thicket

64: Heart of a Volcano

65: Heart of an Evil Kingdom

66: Hovering off the Ground (Roll again to see above what.)

67: In a Fallow Field

68: In a Frozen Mountain Valley

69: In a Lost Stretch of a Jungle

70: In a Major City's Sewers

71: In a Modest Town's Sewers

72: In a Mountain Valley

73: In Another Plane/Dimension

74: Inside of a Hidden Ship's Cove

75: Inside of a High Plateau

76: Inside of a Huge Cavern

77: Inside of a Large Garden

78: Inside of a Large Local Park

79: Inside of a Major City

80: Inside of a Mine

81: Inside of a Modest Town

82: Inside of a Ruined Tower

83: Inside of a Series of Caverns

84: Inside of a Stone Grotto

85: Inside of an Excavation Site

86: Inside of an Iceberg

87: Inside of the Dam of a River or Lake

88: Just Outside of a Fortified Keep

89: Just Outside of a Major City

90: Just Outside of a Modest Town

91: Just Outside of a Remote Village

92: Just Outside of a Ruined Tower

93: Just Outside of a Small Hamlet

94: On a Coastal Island

95: On a Faraway Continent (Roll again for specifics.)

96: On a Remote Island

97: On a Remote Peninsula

98: On a Remote Stretch of Coastland

99: On a Remote Stretch of River

100: On an Iceberg

Lighting (d20)

Though many dungeon inhabitants have ways to see in the dark, others may depend on light sources to see in the darkness below. Even subterranean peoples use light sources for a variety of reasons, including dealing with light-dependent peoples. Roll on this table to generate one or more interesting sources of light for the dungeon.

1: Torches, smoky and sputtering

2: Torches, average

3: Torches, clean and high quality

4: Braziers

5: Candles, unmounted

6: Candles, mounted on simple holders

7: Candles, mounted on handheld candlesticks

8: Candles, mounted on shoulder-height candleholders

9: Candles, mounted in lanterns

10: Candles, mounted on candelabras

11: Candles, mounted on hanging chandeliers

12: Candles, mounted in hurricane glasses

13: Candles, mounted in colored/tinted hurricane glasses

14: Oil lamps

15: Mirrors

16: Bioluminescent plant life

17: Bioluminescent fungi

18: Bioluminescent mold

19: Bioluminescent animals/insects

20: Magical Lighting (See page 36.)

Magical Lighting (d20)

Sometimes ordinary light sources just aren't fancy enough. Ancient, powerful, or magically attuned dungeons might be equipped with enchanted methods of lighting their rooms and halls—if they require light at all. Roll on this table to generate an interesting and exciting means of magical luminescence.

1: Enchanted Mirrors

2: Eternal Candles (Normal Color)

3: Eternal Candles (Strange Light)

4: Eternal Lantern (Normal Light)

5: Eternal Lantern (Strange Light)

6: Eternal Torches (Green Light)

7: Eternal Torches (Normal Light)

8: Eternal Torches (Strange Light)

9: Floating Faerie Lights

10: Glowing Ceiling

11: Glowing Mounted Domes

12: Glowing Orbs

13: Glowing Runes

14: Glowing Wall

15: Illusory Light

16: Magic Glow Bugs

17: Magic Glow Toads

18: Radiant Holy Light

19: Sourceless Ambient Light

20: Transparent Ceiling

Temperature (d20)

Even indoors and underground, a dungeon has weather of its own kind, usually determined by the dungeon's temperature. It's likely that the dungeon has a temperature at least similar to that of the surrounding ecology, but the dungeon may be warmer or colder for a variety of reasons. Your dungeon might be cool and insulated against the desert heat, or streams of lava may keep an otherwise-frozen dungeon warm. Roll on this table to generate a temperature for your dungeon.

Temperature	Description
1: Freezing	Almost uninhabitable, the extreme cold of the environment is a major concern for exploration. Numbness, uncontrolled shivering, and frostbite may result.
2–3: Cold	Exploration takes a toll, slowly exhausting and chilling characters who spend days or even hours without proper gear.
4–7: Cool	Mostly fine for exploration, but prolonged rest and habitation may result in sickness or other health concerns.
8–13: Moderate	Ideal for exploration and adventuring and offers no penalties or benefits.
14–17: Warm	Mostly fine for exploration but can become tiring for characters in thick metal armor or for those carrying heavy loads.
18–19: Hot	Exploration takes a toll, slowly exhausting and dehydrating characters who spend days or even hours without proper shelter.
20: Smoldering	Almost uninhabitable, the heat of the environment is a major concern for exploration. Extreme perspiration, delirium, and heat stroke may result.

Air Quality (d8)

The air quality of your dungeon may impede or even aid exploration by the party in a number of ways. Breathing conditions, concealment opportunities, and many other circumstances may be dictated by the prevailing weather conditions within the halls and corridors. Roll on this table to generate an interesting quality of the air in your dungeon, applying the following modifiers based on the dungeon's temperature:

Freezing: +0 | **Cold:** +1 | **Cool:** +2 | **Moderate:** +3 | **Warm:** +5 | **Hot:** +6 | **Smoldering:** +7

Air Quality	Description
1: Frosty	A heavy layer of frost covers many surfaces of the dungeon. The frost may conceal details and features, compromise the balance of characters, and cause doors and latches to stick.
2: Foggy	A thick fog fills the rooms and corridors of the dungeon. At its thickest, this fog obscures both the party and their enemies, aiding those who use it to gain the element of surprise.
3: Biting Wind	A freezing-cold wind rushes through the dungeon, slicing those who encounter it with its dagger-like cold and force. Creatures must be wary to avoid being pushed around by the freezing wind.
4: Misty	A thin mist lightly obscures the dungeon, making details hard to pick out from a distance. Hiding is aided by the mist, as faraway objects and people can be easily mistaken.
5: Damp	The air is wet and moist in the dungeon, impacting the party's ability to rest without their gear and boots getting soggy. Certain terrain may be softer or more flexible, and most surfaces are slippery, impacting climbing and balance.
6: Low Mist	A low mist clings to the floor of the dungeon. The mist conceals smaller characters and objects close to the ground. Floor-based traps and triggers are especially difficult to pick out.
7: Drafty	A slightly cool wind runs through the dungeon, circulating the air and making a low moaning noise. The sound might be useful to mask the shuffle of movement, or to create unsettling audible effects.
8: Clear	The air is clear in the dungeon and offers no obstacles to sight, smell, or other senses.
9: Windy	A slightly warm wind runs through the dungeon, circulating the air and making a low howling noise. The sound might be useful to mask the vibration of movement, or to create unsettling audible effects.

Air Quality	Description
10: Dry	The air is dry and crisp and has very little moisture. It presents no obstacles other than making the party a bit thirsty, depleting their stores of water at a slightly accelerated rate.
11: High Smoke	A layer of smoke clings to the upper ceiling of this dungeon. The smoke only interferes with flying creatures and very tall characters, though others smell the scent of the smoke almost exclusively. Ceiling-based traps and triggers are especially difficult to pick out.
12: Hazy	A haze in the air of the dungeon makes objects in the distance shimmer and distort. Hiding at a distance is aided by the haze, while attacks are hindered by the distortion effect.
13: Heavy Wind	A roaring hot wind rushes through the dungeon, blasting those who encounter it with its open-furnace-like heat and force. Creatures must be wary against the heated wind.
14: Smoky	Thick smoke fills the rooms and corridors of the dungeon. This makes both seeing and breathing difficult, especially as one draws closer to the source of the smoke.
15: Steamy	Steam fills the air, resulting in slick condensation on most surfaces, providing concealment and cover, and even causing burns to those who move through its hottest points.

Water Sources (d20)

Most dungeon inhabitants require fresh water sources. Even plants and other simpler entities like oozes and fungi still require water, and sentient species often find it necessary to get creative in how they source fresh water in dungeons, where it is typically scarce. Roll on this table to generate one or more interesting sources of water for the dungeon.

1: Canals

2: Condensation

3: Desalination

4: Fungi Extraction

5: Groundwater Pump

6: Lake

7: Magical Source

8: Magical Spells

9: Meltwater Harvest

10: Plant Extraction

11: Pond

12: Pool

13: Rain Collection

14: Reservoir

15: River

16: Rivulet

17: Spring

18: Stream

19: Waterfall

20: Well

Food Sources (d20)

Most dungeon inhabitants require food sources. Even the undead, fiends, or other supernatural entities may require a form of sustenance, which must be procured and harvested by a means similar to that of ordinary food. Roll on this table to generate one or more interesting sources of food for the dungeon.

Source	Description
1: Cannibalism	The dungeon inhabitants sustain themselves by devouring the weak or dead amongst their number.
2: Captives	Captives are brought back alive to the dungeon, due to either necessity or preference. Prisoners may last a long time as they are fattened, tenderized, or preserved for future meals.
3: Complex Farms	A farming system that uses technology and knowledge of advanced farming techniques sustains crop growth within the dungeon.
4: Egg Harvest	The eggs of birds, reptiles, and even sentient egg-laying peoples within the dungeon or out in the surrounding region provide sustenance for the dungeon inhabitants.
5: Enormous Prey Animal(s)	The dungeon inhabitants eat by hunting or harvesting the flesh from a single self-regenerating beast, or a herd of enormous beasts.
6: Fishing	Fish that are swimming through or living in bodies of water within the dungeon or out in the surrounding region are caught for survival.
7: Fruit Harvest	Berries, crabapples, grapes, and other fruits or wild vegetables are harvested within the dungeon or out in the surrounding region.
8: Fungal Farms	The dungeon inhabitants cultivate mushrooms and other fungi of nutritional value using a simple farming system.
9: Hunted Insects	Catching and harvesting insects, spiders, grubs, worms, roaches, and other tiny creepy crawlers offer the best chance of survival.
10: Hunted Vermin	Catching rats, mice, squirrels, and other vermin, which the dungeon inhabitants attempt to cook as best as possible, provide the opportunity of survival.
11: Large Prey Animals	The dungeon inhabitants hunt and likely cook deer, wild bison, bears, and other large prey animals within the dungeon or out in the surrounding region.
12: Livestock	Livestock—either well-known breeds, or else unique livestock better suited to life in the dungeon—are herded, cultivated, and/or domesticated here.

Source	Description
13: Magical Farms	A farming system uses magic to generate the necessary life force, light, water, or nutrition to sustain crop growth.
14: Magical Growth	A magical self-replenishing food source, such as a fountain of nourishing water, a table that produces never-ending meals, or a trough of limitless nutrient paste, allows for survival in this dungeon.
15: Moss/Lichen	The dungeon inhabitants survive as best they can on the barely nutritional moss or lichen that grows in the dungeon, likely on surfaces near water sources.
16: Nut Harvest	Acorns, chestnuts, and other nuts are harvested within the dungeon or out in the surrounding region.
17: Organic Growth	The dungeon inhabitants survive as best they can by harvesting mushrooms, mold, shoots, wild plants, and other growths that occur naturally in the dungeon, likely on surfaces near water sources.
18: Simple Farms	A simple farming system produces basic crops and plants of nutritional value.
19: Small Prey Animals	Birds, rabbits, foxes, and other small prey animals within the dungeon or out in the surrounding region are hunted and cooked.
20: Victims	The dungeon inhabitants devour their slain enemies, including enemies who may have only become such after being purposefully and repeatedly hunted for food.

Noises (d100)

The eerie, echoing, often distant sounds that fill dungeons are a key feature of their individual atmosphere, as well as clues or hints of what might be ahead. Roll on this table to generate a unique sound to surprise or incentivize characters with, or just to keep things interesting during a rest. You might also generate a particular persistent sound to fill the dungeon; characters can use this sound to navigate closer to or away from the source of the noise.

1: Alarm Bells

2: Banging

3: Barking

4: Belches

5: Bellowing

6: Bird Calls

7: Booming

8: Buzzing

9: Chanting

10: Chiming

11: Chirping

12: Clanking

13: Clashing

14: Clattering

15: Clicking

16: Clinking

17: Coughs

18: Creaks

19: Croaks

20: Crying

21: Distorted Echoes

22: Dripping

23: Drumming

24: Fighting Noises

25: Fire Crackling

26: Footsteps Ahead

27: Footsteps Approaching

28: Footsteps Receding

29: Footsteps to the Side

30: Gasps

31: Gibbering

32: Giggling

33: Gong Sounding

34: Grating

35: Grinding

36: Groans

37: Growls

38: Grunts

39: Hammering

40: Hissing

41: Horn Sounding

42: Howls

43: Humming

44: Jingling

45: Knocking

46: Laughter

47: Mining Sounds

48: Moaning

49: Murmurs

50: Music (Ethereal)

51: Music (High Quality)

52: Music (Low Quality)

53: Rattling

54: Ringing

55: Roars

56: Rustling

57: Scrabbling

58: Scraping

59: Scratching

60: Screams

61: Scuttling

62: Shouts

63: Shrieks

64: Shuffling

65: Slamming

66: Slithering

67: Slurping

68: Smashing

69: Snapping

70: Sneezing

71: Snoring

72: Sobbing

73: Splashing

74: Splintering

75: Squeaking

76: Squeals

77: Swooshing

78: Tapping

79: Tearing

80: Thudding

81: Thumps

82: Ticking

83: Tinkling

84: Trilling

85: Trumpet Sounding

86: Twanging

87: Voices Arguing

88: Voices Cursing

89: Voices Speaking

90: Wailing

91: Wheezing

92: Whining

93: Whirring

94: Whispers

95: Whistling (Instrumental)

96: Whistling (Vocal)

97: Wind Blowing

98: Wings Flapping

99: Yapping

100: Yelps

Odors (d20)

Darkness and distant sounds can feel oppressive, but nothing matches the smell of a dungeon for assaulting the senses of the characters. Some odors might mask the presence of certain creatures, while others might hint at their presence. Smells can conceal the party's intrusion or even impede their progress. Roll on this table to generate a unique set of smells for your dungeon, or for a particular area of your dungeon.

1: Acrid

2: Chlorine

3: Dank

4: Earthy

5: Manure

6: Metallic

7: Moldy

8: Musty

9: Ozone

10: Putrid

11: Rotting Flesh

12: Rotting Vegetation

13: Salty

14: Smoky

15: Stale

16: Sulfurous

17: Sweaty

18: Urine

19: Waste/Leavings

20: Wet

Dungeon Facade (d20)

In some ways, the front entrance of the dungeon is the most important part. It sets the tone for the whole expedition and, more often than not, hints at the dangers to come. At the very least, it sets the expectations of the adventurers. Roll on this table to generate a fun and curiosity-provoking facade for your dungeon.

Dungeon Facade	Description
1: Archway	A carved archway with no doors or obvious barriers adorns the entrance of the dungeon. There is a capstone or keystone at the apex of the arch, which could collapse (or be rigged to collapse) the entire entrance if its structural integrity were somehow sabotaged.
2: Bridge	The party must safely cross a bridge (see page 101) to reach the front entrance and enter the dungeon. The dungeon inhabitants likely use the bridge as a dangerous bottleneck.
3: Cataclysmic Wound	This front entrance is a savage and ragged wound in the earth, stone, or other material forming the dungeon, which is likely unstable and prone to collapse. The wound was created by a large-scale cataclysm such as an earthquake, divine intervention, explosion, or other phenomenon that smote the place long ago.
4: Cave Mouth	A naturally formed cave mouth may be ominous and obvious as the dungeon entrance, or it may require special knowledge and skills to locate the correct cave.
5: Choice of Doors	A choice of multiple doors (see page 110), likely between two and five options, makes up this front entrance. There may be more than one correct entrance, but at least one of the doors is a decoy that likely traps and eliminates intruders who don't know the location of the true entrance.

Dungeon Facade	Description
6: Climbing Ascent/ Descent	A climb, either up or down a wall, cliff, or ruin of great height, is required to reach this dungeon.
7: Defensible Porch	A large extended porch-like structure or other raised fortification allows the dungeon's inhabitants to effectively defend the entrance from advantageous positions.
8: Drop Descent	A sheer drop, with no stairs or climbing options, leads into the dungeon. Those seeking to enter the dungeon must find a way to lower a rope or otherwise safely descend to the dungeon floor below.
9: Enormous Skull	This front entrance has been placed in the mouth, eye socket, or other opening in a huge skull. The skull might have been carved from stone or another material, or it might be the skull of an enormous monster or godlike being.
10: Gateway/ Portcullis	A gate, portcullis, or other non-door barrier, likely made of metal or some other resilient material, guards this front entrance. The gate must be pushed or lifted open by sheer force to get past, or a winch or other mechanism must be located and accessed (likely on the other side of the gate).
11: Huge Doors	This front entrance is a massive set of ordinary doors (see page 110). The doors may be so large that moving them takes a particularly heroic effort, or the work of multiple individuals.
12: Huge Staircase	A massive staircase of monolithic proportions leads up or down into the dungeon. It might be intended for human-size individuals and is simply grand in scope, or it might be a proportional staircase intended for particularly large entities.
13: Lift	A mechanical or magical lift raises or lowers individuals into the heights or depths of the dungeon. It may do so automatically, or it may require some force, effort, or source of power to run properly.
14: Long and Winding Stairs	A long, winding, and likely treacherous set of steps must be climbed up or down into the dungeon. Individually the steps are not especially slippery or dangerous, but the long, tedious climb presents many opportunities for individuals to lose focus and make a fatal misstep.
15: Massive Corpse	This front entrance has been placed in the corpse of a gargantuan fallen beast, machine, deity, or other entity. The corpse may be reduced to bones or other solid components (possibly even stone or other inorganic matter), or it may still be rotting, or it may have been supernaturally preserved since the moment of demise.

Dungeon Facade	Description
16: Mineshaft Entrance	This front entrance was built to serve as the access point for a mining or other industrial operation. There are likely tools and piles of ore and rubble scattered around the entrance, as well as minecart tracks and at least one minecart for the party to use as they see fit.
17: Ordinary-Size Door	This seemingly ordinary door (see page 110) may not present an issue when trying to open it, but the door is difficult to spot from a distance.
18: Portal Opening	Rather than a physical opening, a magical or supernatural portal leads into the dungeon. It may be located near the dungeon itself, or it may actually be far away or even on another world entirely.
19: Staircase	A staircase, likely in a stairwell, leads down into the depths of the dungeon.
20: Stepping Stones	A set of stepping stones might be trapped or spaced in such a way as to present an obstacle to those attempting to enter the dungeon.

Entrance Defenses (d20)

It is all too likely that the front entrance of a dungeon will be guarded, warded, or otherwise defended by some powerful means intended to drive off the cowardly and make even the bravest adventurer second-guess proceeding any further. Roll on this table to generate an exciting and suspense-creating defensive measure for your dungeon's entrance that is sure to put the party on their toes.

Defense	Description
1: All-Seeing Eye	An enchanted orb, fireball, or other eye-like sphere allows occupants of the dungeon to be alerted to approaching enemies from potentially miles away.
2: Arrow Slits	Arrow slits built into the walls allow occupants of the dungeon to spy and use a defensive position to fire upon enemies who they spot approaching the entrance.
3: Concealment	This front entrance has been concealed, hidden, or otherwise obscured (see page 118) by the dungeon's original builders, or it might be an addition of the current inhabitants.
4: Covered Positions	A retaining wall, large fortification, rocky outcropping, crenellations, or some other defensive measure allows the dungeon's defenders to easily take cover or get out of the line of fire while repelling invaders.
5: Double Doors/Watergate	Two sets of doors are designed to funnel, contain, and possibly even trap intruders between them.
6: Hard to Find	This front entrance has been placed in such a way as to prevent it from being easily located or noticed, even by those deliberately seeking it.
7: Locked Doors	A key or lock-picking skills are required to enter this locked (see page 121) front entrance.
8: Lookout Post	One or more buildings, huts, or dungeon rooms are located near the entrance, from which lookouts can see approaching enemies from potentially dozens of feet away.
9: Lookout Tower	One or more elevated lookout towers are built outside of this front entrance, which allows lookouts to see approaching enemies from potentially hundreds of feet away.
10: Multiple Traps	Multiple smaller traps dissuade, drive off, or kill would-be intruders.
11: Murder Holes	An upper floor (called a hoarding) allows guards to shoot and pour unfortunate substances down upon intruders.

Defense	Description
12: None	This front entrance has no defenses, but that won't prevent the party from worrying.
13: Outer Walls	One or more sets of outer walls, like the walls of a keep or a castle, protect this front entrance. The dungeon inhabitants may leave the walls unguarded or may have some troops on the wall to see and defend against approaching enemies.
14: Precarious Approach	The top or bottom of a particularly precarious staircase, dangerous climb, narrow bridge, or other approach is designed to end the party's adventure before it ever begins. Completing the climb without magic or aid is far from guaranteed.
15: Relay Lookouts	One or more lookouts on duty have the job of running to alert the next group of lookouts, and so on, until the whole dungeon is alerted. The initial lookouts must be eliminated to prevent a chain reaction.
16: Sealed Doors	This front entrance has been sealed, shut, or otherwise barred (see page 122).
17: Single Guardian	A single massive guardian, likely one who is trapped, bound, or otherwise coerced into service as a guardian, or who is simply too destructive to be allowed any closer to the dungeon and its occupants, guards this front entrance.
18: Single Trap	A single powerful trap dissuades, drives off, or kills would-be intruders.
19: Wandering Guardians	Wandering guardians may prevent access to the dungeon or cause a conflict that reveals the party's approach.
20: Wandering Patrols	Wandering patrols of dungeon occupants or minions prevent access to the dungeon or cause a conflict that reveals the party's approach.

Secret Entrances (d12)

While a front entrance may be well guarded, many dungeons come equipped with an alternate means of entering and exiting. Typically, such secret entrances are extremely well hidden, either by craft or by circumstance, given the huge defensive liability they present. Most secret entrances are never discovered until well after they would be most useful. Secret entrances may bypass just the guards and defenses or may cut around huge sections or entire floors of the dungeon; they may even lead straight to the villain's personal chambers! Roll on this table to generate an exciting and clever secret entrance for your dungeon.

Entrance	Description
1: Collapsed Tunnel	Once an ordinary means of entry into the dungeon, this entrance has clearly collapsed and been rendered impassable for some time. Powerful magic, brute strength coupled with engineering skills, or other means might be employed to make this tunnel traversable again.
2: Drainage Chute	This classic "sewer entrance" allows access to the dungeon at the cost of the heroes' comfort and hygiene. Bad smells and disease might be a concern, but greater hazards, such as locked grates, slipping, drowning in muck, or being crushed by falling garbage, may present even more of an obstacle.
3: Escape Passage	Designed to allow the inhabitants of the dungeon to escape their lair undetected by besieging forces, this entrance likely leads directly into the high-priority sections of the dungeon (possibly even the villain's own quarters). Thus, the exterior opening of the passage is especially well concealed by the intended users.
4: Infiltration Tunnel	Dug or built by spies or other enemies attempting to infiltrate the dungeon, this tunnel's exterior opening is carefully constructed. The interior opening is rough, unstable, narrow, and likely hidden or concealed within the dungeon.
5: Invasion Tunnel	This entrance was dug or built by an invading or besieging force that was able to work en masse to dig this massive tunnel. While the exterior opening is well constructed, the interior opening is rough, unstable, and likely the site of a massive battle.
6: Magical Opening	This entrance is supernaturally sealed (see page 122) and requires some special key, password, or secret to be opened. Thus, it does not see frequent use by the dungeon inhabitants and may not be guarded (or might be forgotten entirely).

Entrance	Description
7: Portal/Rift	Supernatural in nature, this entrance breaks the laws of space and physics to allow passage to and from the dungeon at a distance. It might be incredibly far away from the dungeon itself and may or may not have been intentionally created by the dungeon inhabitants.
8: Sally Port	This fortified side-door into the dungeon allowed the original builders to "sally forth"—that is, emerge by surprise and attack forces besieging the front entrance. The sally port is typically guarded, locked, and sealed by multiple means, and its material is reinforced against breakdown (see page 111).
9: Underground River	A naturally formed passage carved out by a river, stream, or rivulet of water flows beneath or through the dungeon. Parts of the river may be accessible from above ground outside the dungeon; otherwise, parties must locate a way down to the river's subterranean level to use this entrance.
10: Underwater Channel	An otherwise ordinary body of water, which is likely deep or opaque enough to hide the opening, conceals this entrance. Traversing the channel may require the means to hold one's breath for long periods, squeeze through narrow gaps, and possibly contend with a current.
11: Ventilation Chimney	This entrance is designed to allow breathable air into the dungeon, or smoke, chemical smog, or other gasses out of the dungeon. It is likely uncomfortably narrow, and the moist or smoky exhalations may interfere with attempts to climb in or out.
12: Vertical Descent	A cliff, waterfall, or other precipice is judged too difficult to be a useful entrance for the dungeon inhabitants and is likely unguarded by them. It will require special equipment, powers, or endurance to survive the descent.

Rooms & Halls

Room Sizes (d100)

Chambers and rooms come in all shapes and sizes. Some are vast underground cathedrals, fantastic in scope, while others are small even for a water closet. Roll on this table to generate the size and dimensions of a particular dungeon room.

1–2: Closet (5 x 5' square)

3–5: Tiny (10 x 10' square)

6–7: Tiny Circle (10' circle)

8–9: Tiny Octagon (10 x 10' octagon)

10–12: Cozy (15 x 15' square)

13–14: Cozy Circle (15' circle)

15: Cozy Octagon (15 x 15' octagon)

16–18: Small Square (20 x 20' square)

19: Small Rectangle (15 x 20' rectangle)

20: Small Rectangle (15 x 25' rectangle)

21: Small Rectangle (15 x 30' rectangle)

22: Small Rectangle (15 x 35' rectangle)

23: Small Rectangle (15 x 40' rectangle)

24: Small Rectangle (20 x 25' rectangle)

25: Small Rectangle (20 x 30' rectangle)

26: Small Rectangle (20 x 35' rectangle)

27: Small Rectangle (20 x 40' rectangle)

28–29: Small Circle (20' circle)

30–31: Small Octagon (20 x 20' octagon)

32: Small Trapezoid (20 x 25' trapezoid)

33: Small Trapezoid (20 x 30' trapezoid)

34: Small Trapezoid (20 x 35' trapezoid)

35: Small Trapezoid (20 x 40' trapezoid)

36–40: Medium Square (30 x 30' square)

41: Medium Rectangle (25 x 30' rectangle)

42: Medium Rectangle (25 x 35' rectangle)

43: Medium Rectangle (25 x 40' rectangle)

44: Medium Rectangle (25 x 45' rectangle)

45: Medium Rectangle (25 x 50' rectangle)

46: Medium Rectangle (30 x 35' rectangle)

47: Medium Rectangle (30 x 40' rectangle)

48: Medium Rectangle (30 x 45' rectangle)

49: Medium Rectangle (30 x 50' rectangle)

50: Medium Rectangle (30 x 55' rectangle)

51: Medium Rectangle (30 x 60' rectangle)

52–54: Medium Circle (30' circle)

55: Medium Octagon (30 x 30' octagon)

56: Medium Trapezoid (30 x 35' trapezoid)

57: Medium Trapezoid (30 x 40' trapezoid)

58: Medium Trapezoid (30 x 45' trapezoid)

59: Medium Trapezoid (30 x 50' trapezoid)

60: Medium Trapezoid (30 x 55' trapezoid)

61: Medium Trapezoid (30 x 60' trapezoid)

62–65: Spacious Square (40 x 40' square)

66: Spacious Rectangle (35 x 40' rectangle)

67: Spacious Rectangle (35 x 45' rectangle)

68: Spacious Rectangle (35 x 50' rectangle)

69: Spacious Rectangle (35 x 55' rectangle)

70: Spacious Rectangle (35 x 60' rectangle)

71: Spacious Rectangle (35 x 65' rectangle)

72: Spacious Rectangle (35 x 70' rectangle)

73: Spacious Rectangle (40 x 45' rectangle)

74: Spacious Rectangle (40 x 50' rectangle)

75: Spacious Rectangle (40 x 55' rectangle)

76: Spacious Rectangle (40 x 60' rectangle)

77: Spacious Rectangle (40 x 65' rectangle)

78: Spacious Rectangle (40 x 70' rectangle)

79: Spacious Rectangle (40 x 75' rectangle)

80: Spacious Rectangle (40 x 80' rectangle)

81-83: Spacious Circle (40' circle)

84: Spacious Octagon (40 x 40' octagon)

85: Spacious Trapezoid (40 x 45' trapezoid)

86: Spacious Trapezoid (40 x 50' trapezoid)

87: Spacious Trapezoid (40 x 55' trapezoid)

88: Spacious Trapezoid (40 x 60' trapezoid)

89: Spacious Trapezoid (40 x 65' trapezoid)

90: Spacious Trapezoid (40 x 70' trapezoid)

91: Spacious Trapezoid (40 x 75' trapezoid)

92: Spacious Trapezoid (40 x 80' trapezoid)

93-95: Large Square (50 x 50' square)

96-97: Open Square (60 x 60' square)

98-99: Vast Square (70 x 70' square)

100: Majestic Square (80 x 80' square)

Floors (d100)

Not every dungeon has nice solid stone for adventurers to walk upon through its rooms and halls. Roll on this table to generate the nature of the floors for a particular dungeon, dungeon section, or room.

1: Molten Lava

2–3: Slime

4–5: Stagnant Water

6–7: Running Water

8: Jagged Rocks

9: Slippery Ice

10: Hardened Lava

11–13: Light Rubble

14–17: Mud

18: Sharp Crystals

19: Uneven Crystals

20–22: Loose Sand

23–26: Loose Soil

27–29: Loose Gravel

30–32: Dense Rubble

33: Wire Mesh

34–38: Earth

39–41: Rotting Wood

42–44: Rough Wood

45–48: Polished Wood

49–51: Natural Stone

52–56: Uneven Stone

57–64: Hewn Stone

65–68: Smooth Stone

69–71: Polished Stone

72–75: Uneven Flagstones

76–82: Flagstones

83–86: Ceramic Tiles

87–88: Mosaic Tiles

89–91: Marble Tiles

92–95: Metal

96–97: Metal Grate

98: Polished Obsidian

99: Mirror

100: Magical Glass

Ceilings (d100)

Dungeon ceilings can be featureless and ordinary, while others are irregular or have unique features that conceal traps and dangers. Roll on this table to generate the nature of the ceilings for a particular dungeon, dungeon section, or room.

1: Dripping Slime

2—3: Carved Ice (Icicles)

4: Sharp Crystals

5: Uneven Crystals

6—11: Packed Earth

12—15: Rotting Wood

16—20: Rough Wood

21—24: Polished Wood

25—30: Reinforced Wood

31—39: Natural Stone (Stalactites)

40—49: Uneven Stone

50—62: Hewn Stone

63—77: Smooth Stone

78—81: Polished Stone

82—87: Stone Masonry

88—92: Reinforced Stone Masonry

93—96: Metal

97—98: Metal Grate

99: Mirror

100: Magical Glass

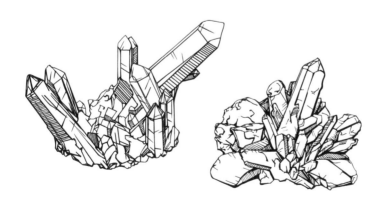

Walls (d100)

Dungeon walls can be as ordinary as stone masonry or as strange as a maze of mirrors. Roll on this table to generate the nature of the walls for a particular dungeon, dungeon section, or room.

1: Paper

2–3: Jagged Rocks

4: Carved Ice

5: Hardened Lava

6–8: Packed Rubble

9–11: Packed Mud

12: Sharp Crystals

13: Uneven Crystals

14–21: Packed Earth

22–25: Rotting Wood

26–30: Rough Wood

31–33: Polished Wood

34–37: Reinforced Wood

38–41: Natural Stone

42–45: Rough Stone

46–51: Hewn Stone

52–59: Smooth Stone

60–65: Polished Stone

66–75: Stone Masonry

76–83: Superior Stone Masonry

84–90: Reinforced Stone Masonry

91–95: Metal

96: Magically Enhanced Masonry

97: Reinforced Glass

98: Mirror

99: Magical Force (Visible)

100: Magical Force (Invisible)

Room Quality (d10)

Dungeons often have a chaotic history. Whole rooms and sections of the structure might be ruined by environmental or combat-related catastrophes. Roll on this table to generate the quality of construction in a particular dungeon, dungeon section, or dungeon room.

Quality	Description
1: Demolished	Utterly destroyed, with hazards in the form of clutter, precarious footing, or even the chance of floor or ceiling collapse, this room cannot be used for its original function—if the adventurers can even discern what that might have been.
2: Wrecked	This room is badly damaged, and its crumbling architecture may present hazards to those who would traverse the space. It likely cannot be used for its original function.
3: Decrepit	Aspects of the architecture or furnishings of this room are at the point of collapse or destruction. It may still be functional for its original purpose, but at minimum requires minor repairs or a thorough cleaning to be used once more.
4: Flooded	Flooding water or other moisture-related damage has weakened the foundations of this room, leaving puddles, cracks, and mold on the walls and floors.
5: Poor	Dirty, cluttered, and not particularly well maintained, this room is serviceable and usable for its original purpose.
6: Livable	This room is not clean and clear, but it is in fairly good condition for an underground dungeon chamber and is somewhat comfortable to sleep or rest in.
7: Clean	The dungeon inhabitants regularly use or even live in this room, which they've recently cleared out and cleaned.
8: Superior	This room is well preserved and even cozy and comfortable, either due to the innate quality of the original architecture or because the dungeon inhabitants have kept the room so well maintained.
9: Elegant	Much of the original architecture of this particularly well-decorated room is in perfect condition, and rules might be in place to keep the dungeon inhabitants from damaging or dirtying it.
10: Majestic	This room is astoundingly well preserved, decadent, and elaborately furnished. It may have been sealed away from the dungeon inhabitants, leading to its current state of preservation. If it could be moved, it might be considered a work of art in its own right.

Room Functions (d100)

A dungeon room is rarely empty (and even then, rarely without good reason). Dungeons can become entire ecosystems, each room playing a vital role in the various defenses, villainous schemes, and lifestyles of the inhabitants. First, determine or refer back to the dungeon type for your dungeon (see page 14). Then, roll on this table to generate a function or purpose for a particular room in your dungeon. See page 72 for a description of the different types of rooms.

Room	Vault	Temple	Barrow	Tomb	Maze
Animal Pen	-	1	1	-	-
Antechamber	1	2	2	1	1–2
Armory	2–3	3	3–5	2–4	3–4
Audience Chamber	-	4	6	5	5
Aviary	-	5	7	6	6
Ballroom	-	-	-	8	-
Banquet Hall	-	-	-	7	-
Barracks	4–5	6	8	9	7
Bath	6	7	9	10	8
Bedroom	7	8	10	11	-
Break Room	8–9	9	11	12	9–10
Catacomb	10	10	12–15	13–15	11–13
Cave	-	-	16–18	16	14
Cell	11–12	11	19–20	17	15–17
Chantry	-	12–13	-	18	-
Chapel	-	14–16	21–22	19–20	18
Chasm	13	-	23–24	-	19
Cistern	14	17	25	21	-
Classroom	-	18	-	-	-
Closet	15–16	19	26	22	20–21
Conjuring Room	17	20	27	23	22
Construction Room	18	21	28	24	23
Containment Room	19	22	29	25	24
Court	20	23	30	26	-

Home	Prison	Mine	Lair	Fortress	Room
1–2	1	1–2	1–2	1–2	Animal Pen
3	2	-	3	3	Antechamber
4	3–5	3–4	4–5	4–6	Armory
5	6	5	6	7–8	Audience Chamber
6	7	6	7	9	Aviary
8	-	-	9	12–13	Ballroom
7	-	-	8	10–11	Banquet Hall
9	8–9	7–8	10–11	14–15	Barracks
10–11	10	9	12	16	Bath
12–14	11	10	13–14	17–18	Bedroom
15	12–13	11–12	15	19	Break Room
16	14–15	13	16–17	20	Catacomb
0	16	14–16	18	-	Cave
17	17–20	17–18	19	21–22	Cell
18	-	-	-	23	Chantry
19	21	19	20	24–25	Chapel
-	22	20–22	21	26	Chasm
-	23	23	-	27	Cistern
20	24	-	22	28	Classroom
21–22	25	24	23	29	Closet
23	26	25	24	30	Conjuring Room
24	27	26–28	25	31	Construction Room
25	28	29	26	32	Containment Room
26	-	-	-	33	Court

Room	Vault	Temple	Barrow	Tomb	Maze
Crypt	21	24–25	31–34	27–31	25–26
Dining Room	-	26	-	-	-
Divination Room	22	27	35	32	27
Dormitory	-	28	-	-	28
Dressing Room	-	29	-	33	-
Factory	23	-	-	-	29
Feast Hall	-	30	36	-	-
Foyer	24	31	-	34	30–31
Gallery	25–27	32–33	-	35–37	32
Game Room	-	-	-	-	-
Garden	-	34–35	37	38	33
Grave	28–29	36	38–42	39–42	34
Graveyard	-	37–38	43–47	43–45	-
Greenhouse	30	39	-	-	35
Guard Chamber	31–33	40	48	46	36–38
Guard Post	34–36	41	49	47	39–41
Gym	-	-	-	-	42
Hall	37–38	42	50	48–49	43–44
Hive	-	-	51–52	50	45
Hoard	39–41	43	53–54	51	46–48
Kennel	42	-	55	-	49
Kitchen	43	44	-	-	-
Laboratory	44	45	56	52	50
Lair	45–46	46	57–58	53–54	51–53
Latrine	-	-	59	55	54
Lavatory	47	47	-	-	-
Library	48–49	48–49	60	56–57	55–56
Living Quarters	50	50	61	58	57
Lounge	-	-	-	59	-
Maze	51–53	51	62–64	60–62	58–62
Meditation Room	54	52	65	63	63
Menagerie	55	53	-	-	64–65

Home	Prison	Mine	Lair	Fortress	Room
27	29	30	27	34	Crypt
28–29	30	31	28	35	Dining Room
30	-	-	29	36	Divination Room
-	31	32	30	-	Dormitory
31	-	-	-	37	Dressing Room
-	32	33	-	38	Factory
-	-	-	31	39	Feast Hall
32	33	-	32	40	Foyer
33–34	-	-	33	41	Gallery
35	34	34	34	-	Game Room
36–37	35	35	35	42	Garden
38–39	-	36	-	-	Grave
40	36–37	37	36	-	Graveyard
41	38	-	37	43	Greenhouse
42	39–40	38	38–39	44–45	Guard Chamber
43–44	41–44	39–40	40–41	46–47	Guard Post
45	45	41	42	48	Gym
46	46	42–43	43	49	Hall
-	47	44–45	44	-	Hive
-	-	46	45–46	50	Hoard
47	48	47	47	51	Kennel
48–49	49	48	48–49	52–53	Kitchen
50	50	49	50	54	Laboratory
51	51–52	50–51	51–54	55	Lair
52	53	52–53	55–56	56	Latrine
53–54	-	-	57	57–58	Lavatory
55–56	54	-	58	59	Library
57	55	54	59	60	Living Quarters
58	-	-	60	-	Lounge
-	56	55	61	-	Maze
59	57	-	62	61	Meditation Room
60–61	58	-	63	62	Menagerie

Room	Vault	Temple	Barrow	Tomb	Maze
Mess Hall	56	-	66	-	66
Mining Area	-	-	67	-	67
Monument	57–60	54–55	68–70	64–67	68–69
Museum	61–63	56–57	71	68–69	70
Nursery	64–65	58	72	70	71
Observatory	-	59–60	73–74	71	72
Office	66–68	61–62	-	-	-
Pantry	69	63	75	-	-
Pit	70	64	76–77	72–73	73
Pool	71	65	78	74–75	74
Portal	72	66	79	76	75
Prison	73–74	67	80	77	76–77
Quarry	-	-	81	-	78
Reception Room	75	68	-	-	79
Refectory	76	69–70	-	78	-
Refuse	-	-	82	79	80
Ritual Chamber	77	71	83	80	81
Robing Room	-	72	-	81	-
Salon	-	-	-	-	-
Sanctum	78	73	84–85	82–83	82
Scrying Chamber	79	74	86	84	83
Shrine	80	75–78	87–89	85–86	84
Sitting Room	81	79	-	-	85
Smithy	-	-	-	-	-
Stable	-	80	90	-	-
Storage Room	82–83	81–82	91	87	86–87
Strong Room	84–85	83	92	88	88–89
Study	-	84–85	-	89	90
Temple	86	86–90	93–94	90–92	91
Theater	-	91	-	-	-
Throne Room	-	92	95	93	92
Torture Chamber	87–88	93	96	94	93

Home	Prison	Mine	Lair	Fortress	Room
-	59	56	64	63	Mess Hall
-	60–61	57–63	65	-	Mining Area
62	62	64	66	64	Monument
63	-	-	-	65	Museum
64	63	65	67–68	66	Nursery
65	64	66	69	67	Observatory
66–67	65	67	70	68	Office
68–69	66	68–69	71–72	69–70	Pantry
-	67–68	70–71	73	-	Pit
70	-	-	74	-	Pool
71	69	72	75	71	Portal
-	70–74	73	76–78	72–73	Prison
-	75–76	74–78	79	-	Quarry
-	77	79	-	74	Reception Room
-	78	-	-	75	Refectory
-	79–80	80	80	-	Refuse
72	81	81	81	76	Ritual Chamber
73	82	-	-	77	Robing Room
74	-	-	-	78	Salon
75	83	82	82	79	Sanctum
76	-	83	83	80	Scrying Chamber
77–78	84–85	84–85	84	81	Shrine
79–80	-	-	-	82	Sitting Room
81	86	86–87	85–86	83–84	Smithy
82	88	88	87	85	Stable
83–85	89–90	89–91	88	86	Storage Room
86–87	91	92–93	89	87	Strong Room
88–89	-	-	90	88	Study
-	-	94	91	89	Temple
90	-	-	92	-	Theater
91	-	-	93	90–91	Throne Room
92	92–93	95	94	92	Torture Chamber

Room	Vault	Temple	Barrow	Tomb	Maze
Training Room	89	94	-	-	94
Trophy Room	90–92	95	97–98	95–96	95
Vault	93–97	96–97	99–100	97–99	96–98
Vestibule	98	98	-	100	-
Well	-	99	-	-	99
Workshop	99	100	-	-	-
Zoo	100	-	-	-	100

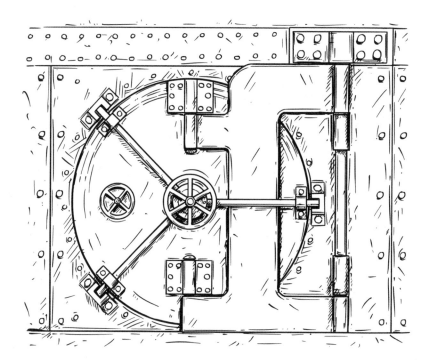

Home	Prison	Mine	Lair	Fortress	Room
93	94	-	95	93	Training Room
94–95	95	-	96–97	94–95	Trophy Room
96	96	96–97	98	96	Vault
97	97	-	-	97	Vestibule
98	98	98	99	98	Well
99	99	99–100	100	99	Workshop
100	100	-	-	100	Zoo

Function	Description
Animal Pen	Domesticated animals, which need little protection or security, are kept here to avoid their wandering or getting hurt.
Antechamber	This room serves as a decorative entrance hall into a larger and more important hall or chamber.
Armory	This room was built to store and maintain weapons and armor, though they may no longer be present or in their original condition.
Audience Chamber	A ruler, authority figure, or other powerful being meets here with large groups and audiences of their loyal subjects to make proclamations, exercise power, and hear pleas.
Aviary	Domesticated messenger birds, ravens, owls, miniature dragons, and other likely intelligent avian or flying creatures are kept and bred here.
Ballroom	Large groups congregate here for dancing, revelry, and other festivities. This room may include a dedicated dance floor, a performance stage for musicians, and an area for drinks and food to be laid out.
Banquet Hall	In this room, a group of loyal subjects and high-ranking individuals could be gathered, seated, and waited upon by servants in comfort, all while celebrating and honoring their leader or ruler.

Function	Description
Barracks	Large group of soldiers use this area to rest and relax in likely close quarters, with small, practical beds, cots, or hammocks designed to efficiently house as many troops as possible.
Bath	Tubs, basins, or pools of water located here are designed to allow one or more individuals to bathe themselves with clean and possibly heated water. This room may also be equipped with lavatory facilities.
Bedroom	One or more dungeon inhabitants may sleep comfortably, enjoy privacy, and keep their personal possessions relatively safe and secure in this room.
Break Room	Dungeon inhabitants use this room to relax, talk, play games, enjoy small meals, and otherwise kick back between their regular shifts of duty.
Catacomb	In this room or series of tunnels, many generations have been laid to rest in small cubbyholes in the wall, across shelves, or stacked up in heaps. It is almost certainly a breeding ground for hauntings.
Cave	This room is nothing more than a naturally formed space in the dungeon, currently being used for no more intentional purpose than cultivating a natural cave ecosystem.
Cell	The dungeon's inhabitants imprison and contain captives in this room, with its sealed or locked door or bars.
Chantry	This room is designed to enhance the visual aesthetics and acoustics of specialized religious services or musical performances wherein choirs or individual singers perform.
Chapel	Small groups of worshippers gather here to worship a deity or pantheon, or many deities and pantheons.
Chasm	This room is long and narrow and immediately drops off into a massive chasm, either natural or created by a large-scale cataclysm (see page 104).
Cistern	Dungeon inhabitants utilize the pool of liquid in this room as a clean and safe water source, possibly only in the case of an emergency or siege.
Classroom	Students receive a general education, learn a particular skill, or are taught a specific cultural or religious message in this room, which is likely equipped with tools and images to aid in this task.
Closet	The safe conditions in this room allow for clothes to be stored, relatively free of moisture, dirt, or hungry moths, either stacked in boxes or hanging from racks.

Function	Description
Conjuring Room	This room houses specialized magical tools used for the purposes of publicly or privately summoning entities and people from faraway lands and other dimensions, and potentially imprisoning them for the summoners' safety.
Construction Room	Tools, building materials, and unfinished portions of the room are everywhere. This room is still largely under construction, and its final intended purpose may not be immediately clear (roll again).
Containment Room	This room contains specialized and potentially dangerous magical equipment with vast amounts of magical or mundane energy, such as electricity, souls, psychic power, or heat.
Court	Here, an authority figure might preside over important decisions and hear pleas while other courtiers stand in attendance.
Crypt	An individual, group, or even generations have been laid to rest in this room's solid tombs and sarcophagi, though it is likely a breeding ground for hauntings.
Dining Room	Here, a large group, family, or community could be gathered, seated, and waited upon by servants while dining well and comfortably amidst fine decor.
Divination Room	Specialized magical tools for the purposes of publicly or privately using divination magic to learn secret information or ancient lore are stored in this room.
Dormitory	A certain group of dungeon inhabitants with particular status sleeps comfortably, enjoys privacy, and keeps their personal possessions relatively safe and secure here.
Dressing Room	This room is equipped to allow a particular individual or group of individuals to dress and attire themselves, prepare themselves for the public, and store their clothing.
Factory	This room accommodates the mass-producing (or approximating mass-production) of certain goods, constructs, or inventions using specialized mechanical or magical equipment.
Feast Hall	In this room, a particularly large group of loyal subjects could be quickly gathered, seated, and waited upon by servants, all while celebrating and honoring their leader or ruler.
Foyer	This decorative entrance hall, likely with seating and other comfortable amenities, leads into a series of different rooms and spaces.

Function	Description
Gallery	Paintings, tapestries, decorations, or other works of art are on display here for their owner or other visitors to appreciate and be impressed by.
Game Room	In this room, individuals may partake in specialized game activities, including tabletop board games, card games, and physical sports.
Garden	The sunlight or nutritional sources in this room allow plants to be cultivated as food, for their magical or mundane herbalistic uses, or simply for their aesthetic value.
Grave	One individual or being has been laid to rest beneath the earth or floor; the room has likely been turned into a shrine or memorial to their life (see page 92).
Graveyard	Many individuals, groups, or even generations have been laid to rest beneath the earth or floor; the room is likely a breeding ground for hauntings.
Greenhouse	A glass roof and/or walls allow plants to be cultivated and thrive in a controlled, sunlit environment for food, for their magical or mundane herbalistic uses, or simply for their aesthetic value.

Function	Description
Guard Chamber	A small to large group of guards can take shifts standing at attention from behind some protective wall, door, or other shielding architecture, with a clear view of the space they are guarding.
Guard Post	One or more guards can stand at attention from behind some protective wall, door, or other shielding architecture, with a clear view of the space they are guarding.
Gym	Exercise and muscle-strengthening equipment is available for dungeon inhabitants (or one particular inhabitant) to maintain and enhance their physique.
Hall	Large groups of individuals may pass through here to move to other parts of the dungeon. While this room is larger than a corridor, it is functionally just another connection between two or more rooms.
Hive	Huge numbers of monstrous dungeon inhabitants or creatures nest here and make their home in close quarters.
Hoard	A large fortune of treasure has been heaped up somewhat haphazardly, with piles of mundane wealth scattered amidst even more valuable prizes and likely protected by overconfident creatures and their traps.
Kennel	In this room, hounds or other hunting beasts are kept eager and hungry (for activity, if not food); the beasts likely require some extra protection and security.

Function	Description
Kitchen	Dungeon inhabitants prepare food here according to whatever methods are necessary given the available food sources and the size of the dungeon's population.
Laboratory	Magical or mundane experiments are performed using the specialized tools, ingredients, or protective measures in this room.
Lair	Here, one monstrous dungeon inhabitant or creature nests and makes their home, likely emerging only to feed or be fed.
Latrine	Dungeon inhabitants go to this room, equipped with a hole or other convenient aperture, to relieve themselves and dispose of waste.
Lavatory	The well-appointed furnishings and equipment in this room allow for comfortably and hygienically disposing of one's bodily waste in a more civilized manner.
Library	A complex and potentially vast collection of books sit on shelves, in stacks, or according to other organization methods. This room could possibly have space available to read at one's leisure.
Living Quarters	A large group of dungeon inhabitants, including commoners and their families, may sleep comfortably and keep their personal possessions relatively safe and secure here.
Lounge	In this room, one or more individuals may relax and enjoy themselves in a friendly, pleasing atmosphere, possibly with accommodations for recreation and food.
Maze	Narrow corridors and tunnels form dead ends, junctions, loops, and other false pathways designed to confuse travelers and likely land them in traps or other danger.
Meditation Room	One or more individuals may gather here to meditate amidst likely sparse furniture and decor, and possibly religious or spiritual iconography.
Menagerie	A handful of interesting or unique animals or other specimens display the power, wealth, and tastes of the collector.
Mess Hall	In this room, a particularly large military force could be quickly gathered, seated, fed and watered, and released once more with minimal chaos and confusion.
Mining Area	Current or former dungeon inhabitants from long ago have dug out and mined this room for the purposes of extracting ore and other valuables from the nearby earth and stone.

Function	Description
Monument	This room, dedicated to the memory of a particular person or event (see page 92), likely contains no remains but serves as a place of reflection for those deeply impacted by the person or event.
Museum	Objects of great historical, sentimental, or cultural value have been put on display here for their owner or other visitors to marvel at. This room is likely under some kind of protection to avoid damage to the objects.
Nursery	Infantile or unhatched creatures live and sleep in this room; they are either juvenile dungeon inhabitants or juvenile versions of the beasts or monsters whom they have domesticated.
Observatory	The specialized tools and machinery in this room may be used to publicly or privately view faraway objects and locations, or the heavens and stars above.
Office	Business, research, and other kinds of work can be performed in privacy with minimal distractions.
Pantry	Foodstuffs, drinks, ingredients, and cooking supplies may be stored here in bulk when necessary, given the dungeon's population.
Pit	This room immediately drops off into a massive pit that is either natural or artificially constructed and roughly square or circular in shape (see page 104).
Pool	Dungeon inhabitants utilize this pool of liquid (full or empty) as a potentially hazardous water source, group bathing space, or recreational swimming area.
Portal	In this room, a permanent magical portal has a clear and dedicated destination, and likely serves as a two-way gateway.
Prison	Dungeon inhabitants imprison and contain large groups of captives in this room's separate or communal cells, likely with some unique quirks (see page 94).
Quarry	This room has been and may still be in the process of being mined for stone, marble, or some other useful construction material.
Reception Room	Large crowds of newly arrived individuals gather, rest, wait, and organize themselves here before proceeding onward.
Refectory	A small group of particular individuals—perhaps the elite or leaders of the dungeon community—gather here for communal meals and relaxation.
Refuse	Garbage, waste, and other refuse is discarded or thrown in this room, which may have a hole or other repository, or garbage may simply be heaped up in piles. It likely contains junk or useful trinkets amidst the refuse.

Function	Description
Ritual Chamber	The specialized magical tools in this room are used to perform individual or communal rituals and ceremonies for harnessing particular powerful or complex magical energies.
Robing Room	This room is used for the task of dressing a particular individual or group of individuals, which may be complex and difficult based on their form and the quality and cut of their clothing.
Salon	This room is used for reception, recreation, relaxation, and possibly the styling of one's hair, clothing, and makeup in comfort.
Sanctum	A villain or other powerful being or authority figure in the dungeon uses this room as a private getaway, headquarters, or place of power.
Scrying Chamber	The specialized magical tools in this room are publicly or privately used for scrying magic to view faraway places and people.
Shrine	A very small group of worshippers, or one single worshipper, may come here to worship a particular faith or deity.
Sitting Room	This room comfortably seats a large group of individuals, in a friendly party atmosphere, with accommodations for recreation and food.

Function	Description
Smithy	Weapons, armor, or other metal equipment is smelted and forged here, likely requiring special equipment, heat sources, and ventilation.
Stable	Domesticated mounts are kept here so that they avoid wandering or getting hurt; the animals are valuable and likely to be guarded and well cared for.
Storage Room	This room is used for storing and preserving goods, loot, and equipment when not in use, and it may be protected or guarded.
Strong Room	Used for storing and protecting a small fortune of treasure or a group of individuals, this room is likely to be securely locked and possibly even trapped.
Study	Used for reading, note taking, and other kinds of academic study, this room includes space for books or other materials to be enjoyed in a leisurely fashion.
Temple	Large groups of worshippers gather here to worship one deity or pantheon, or many deities and pantheons.
Theater	This room holds musical performances, theatrical plays, and other kinds of shows. It includes a staging area with space for the audience and backstage actors nearby.
Throne Room	This room was appointed for a ruler to sit atop their throne, either on display for their adoring subjects or sanctimoniously isolated away. The throne may or may not still be present, but it certainly is (or was) the main feature of the room.
Torture Chamber	Sadistic arts of interrogation are performed here, where torture devices and victims are displayed for prolonged periods of time.
Training Room	Training equipment, target dummies, and obstacle courses are available here for dungeon inhabitants (or one particular inhabitant) to maintain and enhance their skill level and training.
Trophy Room	This room stores and displays an arrangement of competition trophies, hunting trophies, or trophies of victories past, with varying levels of grisliness.
Vault	This room stores and protects a large fortune of treasure, or a particularly valuable prize, and is likely guarded with difficult locks and traps.
Vestibule	Small groups wait in this room for an appointment or meeting while other business is being resolved. It likely includes seating and other comfortable amenities.

Function	Description
Well	This room contains a well with fresh potable water, or itself is filled with fresh potable water, and it likely serves as a useful water source for the inhabitants of the dungeon.
Workshop	This room serves as a construction or repair space for arms and armor, machinery, inventions, or other goods that require specialized tools to build.
Zoo	Exotic animal specimens from across the land, world, or even multiverse are on display here for dungeon inhabitants and other visitors to see and be impressed by.

Room Features (d100)

While they might not all be stuffed to the brim with treasure and danger, a typical dungeon room has at least a few interesting features to distinguish it from other rooms—even rooms with similar or identical functions. Empty rooms in particular feel a bit more exciting when there are a few features to make them stand out and make the party nervous while they rest. Roll on this table to generate one or more unique features for a dungeon room.

1: Alcove

2: Animal Nest

3: Arch

4: Arrow Slit

5: Balcony

6: Bloodstain

7: Broken Door

8: Broken Fountain

9: Broken Furniture

10: Broken Statue (See page 89.)

11: Carved Words

12: Catwalk

13: Ceiling Carving

14: Ceiling Collapse

15: Chandelier

16: Charcoal Bin

17: Chute

18: Claw Marks

19: Cobwebs

20: Cold Spot

21: Collapsed Wall

22: Container (See page 86.)

23: Cracks

24: Crater (Result of Explosion or Collapse)

25: Curtain

26: Deep Pit

27: Dome

28: Dripping Water

29: Dung Heap

30: Dust

31: Fallen Stones

32: Firepit

33: Fireplace

34: Floor Carving

35: Floor Markings

36: Font

37: Forge

38: Fountain

39: Fungus

40: Furniture (See page 85.)

41: Hole

42: Insects

43: Iron Bars

44: Kiln

45: Ledge

46: Loose Masonry

47: Mold

48: Mosaic

49: Mounted Mirror

50: Mud

51: Mysterious Stain

52: Odor (Roll on page 47.)

53: Oven

54: Overhang

55: Painted Ceiling

56: Painted Floor

57: Painted Wall

58: Pedestal

59: Peephole

60: Pen

61: Pillar

62: Pillory

63: Platform

64: Pole

65: Pool

66: Portcullis

67: Puddle of Oil

68: Puddle of Water

69: Ramp

70: Recess

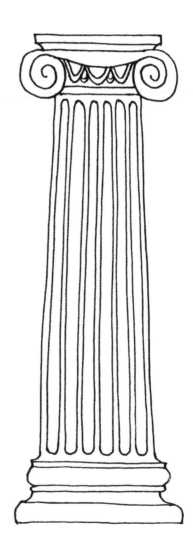

71: Relief Carving

72: Rivulet

73: Rubble Pile

74: Runic Inscriptions

75: Scattered Stones

76: Sconce

77: Scorch Marks

78: Scrawled Words

79: Screen

80: Shallow Pit

81: Shelf

82: Slime

83: Spikes

84: Spilled Oil

85: Spilled Perfume

86: Spilled Spices

87: Splattered Paint

88: Stall

89: Steps

90: Sunken Area

91: Symbol

92: Unidentifiable Odor

93: Unidentifiable Sound

94: Wall Basin

95: Wall Carving

96: Wall Markings

97: Wall-Mounted Chains

98: Wall-Mounted Manacles

99: Well

100: Winch and Pulley

Furniture (d20)

Even the most spartan dungeon rooms and quarters might have the occasional piece of furniture or decoration to make the space a bit more livable. Furnishings can make a dungeon room more interesting and distinctive and give hints as to the room's current function. Furniture may serve as unexpected treasure to particularly ambitious parties, or even as improvised weaponry in the right hands. Roll on this table to generate an interesting piece of treasure to populate a room in your dungeon.

1: Bed

2: Bench

3: Bookcase

4: Brazier

5: Chair

6: Coat Rack

7: Divan

8: Large Table

9: Manger

10: Rack

11: Small Table

12: Spinning Wheel

13: Stool

14: Throne

15: Tiny Table

16: Tripod

17: Trough

18: Tub

19: Unique Table

20: Workbench

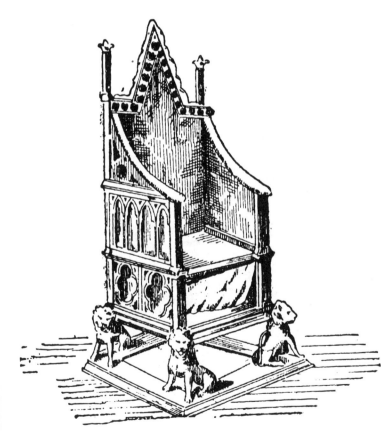

Containers (d20)

Treasure is rarely found scattered around the floor of a dungeon. Loot and possessions with any value are often kept in containers for security and preservation. Roll on this table to generate an interesting container for a dungeon room.

1: Altar

2: Bale of Straw

3: Barrel

4: Box

5: Cage

6: Cart

7: Casket

8: Cauldron

9: Chest

10: Chest of Drawers

11: Clay Pot

12: Crate

13: Cupboard

14: Hay Pile

15: Shrine

16: Trash Pile

17: Urn

18: Vase

19: Wardrobe

20: Weapon Rack

Paintings (d12)

Though they may vary in quality as living spaces, dungeons often become works of art in their own right. The walls, floors, and ceilings of a dungeon might be covered with or even transformed into paintings, tapestries, mosaics, carpets, or other two-dimensional artistic images. These pieces are some of the least portable treasures in a dungeon, being either attached to or part of a dungeon's surface, or else too large or awkward to easily move. Yet their age or historical value might make them the most precious loot of all. Roll on this table to generate a unique work of art for your party to stumble across in a dungeon room or hall.

Painting	Description
1: Abstract Art	This painting depicts mysterious shapes, swirling colors, and other abstract imagery that has no apparent meaning. Secret messages or coded clues may be contained in the painting.
2: Coat of Arms	This coat of arms or crest of a particular family or individual related to the dungeon contains elements that hint at the nature or past of the family or individual.
3: Divine Image	A specific deity or entity of godlike powers is shown in its typical fashion or may have been given a reinterpretation by the painter, reflecting their perspective of the being.
4: Expressionistic	A scene or person has been radically altered, warped, or distorted to capture a particular subjective perspective. It is likely intended to reveal a point of view unique to the painter.
5: Geometric Shapes/Patterns	Regular geometric patterns in fractal, lattice, or even Escherian arrangements contain secret messages or coded clues.
6: Historical Scene	A specific historical scene of great importance to the dungeon or the painter may contain an important clue, historical detail, or other information useful to the party.
7: Impressionistic	This painting depicts a scene or person in such a way as to evoke a particular feeling or mood. The use of light and angles creates an emotion in the viewer that reflects the attitude of the painter.
8: Landscape Scene	The painter has depicted a particular landscape or region of importance to them. It may be the very land where the dungeon is located; the exterior of the dungeon may be featured in the painting itself.

Painting	Description
9: Nature Scene	A scene of natural beauty offers a specific kind of wilderness aesthetic. It may depict the natural world around the dungeon, or that of a specific faraway location.
10: Portrait	This painting depicts the visage of a famous or well-known individual, at least in the context of the dungeon. It may show the depicted individual at an earlier stage of their life, revealing details about their former appearance or even previously unknown family connections.
11: Religious Scene	A specific religious scene of great importance to the dungeon or painter gives insight into the motives and goals of the faith.
12: Structure Scene	A particular building, structure, or cityscape scene depicts the dungeon itself, either in modern times or in its distant past, perhaps at the height of its power. It may depict an important nearby structure or a city of importance to the painter.

Statues/Statuettes (d20)

The inhabitants of dungeons often use stone, or whatever construction material is most available, to create statues large and small. Statues found as dungeon features are often immobile; statues found as treasure are often mobile, at least barely. These statues typically function as tribute, featuring the likenesses of important people and things from the history of the former dungeon occupants, current enemy occupants, or whoever constructed the statue. Roll on this table to generate a unique idea for the likeness represented by a particular statue.

Statues	Description
1: Abstract	This statue is a work of abstract three-dimensional art. The shapes and patterns might contain no significance, or ominously imply ideas in line with the dungeon. The statue's form may even serve as a clue to a puzzle, though this may not be immediately obvious.
2: Beloved Deity	A god, deity, or other divine being that the dungeon inhabitants love and cherish has been depicted as generous and benevolent.
3: Beloved Entity	A spirit, nonhuman entity, or other supernatural being that the dungeon inhabitants love and cherish has been depicted as generous and benevolent.
4: Despised Deity	A god, deity, or other divine being that the dungeon inhabitants hate and despise has been depicted as menacing and dangerous.
5: Despised Leader	A former leader from the dungeon itself or a nearby kingdom or nation that the dungeon inhabitants hate and despise has been depicted as foolish, menacing, or merciless.
6: Feared Entity	Dungeon inhabitants fear a spirit, nonhuman entity, or other supernatural being to the point of exaggerating the features and powers of the entity in its depiction.
7: Feared Foe	Dungeon inhabitants fear an enemy to the point of exaggerating its horrible or dangerous features.
8: Feared Leader	Dungeon inhabitants fear a leader from the dungeon itself or a nearby kingdom or nation to the point of exaggerating the leader's features and authority.
9: Feared Monster	Dungeon inhabitants fear a monster or other great beast to the point of exaggerating the features and powers of the creature.
10: Important Cultural Leader	This statue depicts a leader from the dungeon itself or a nearby kingdom or nation who brought about a cultural revolution or began a philosophical movement of some kind.

Statues	Description
11: Important Hero	This statue depicts a great and famous hero from a nearby kingdom or nation, possibly a former character of one of the players, who accomplished some important deed or deeds in the past.
12: Important Noble	This statue depicts a leader from a nearby kingdom or nation who held an office or title of significance and importance.
13: Important Recent Leader	The leader depicted by this statue is from the dungeon itself or a nearby kingdom or nation. Until very recently, they led a powerful faction. Many of the leader's most zealous devotees still live nearby.
14: Important Spiritual Leader	This statue depicts a leader from the dungeon itself or a nearby kingdom or nation who brought about a new kind of worship or faith or reformed the practices of the current religion.
15: Important Warrior	This statue depicts a warrior, soldier, or general from a nearby kingdom or nation who accomplished some great victory, conquest, or honorable defeat of great regional importance.
16: Mythological Figure	The hero, leader, or other figure depicted by this statue did not actually exist but is a common part of the legends and myths of a particular kingdom or nation.
17: Respected Deity	The dungeon inhabitants have depicted a god, deity, or other divine being whom they cautiously respect as powerful and aloof.
18: Respected Entity	The dungeon inhabitants have depicted a spirit, nonhuman entity, or other supernatural being whom they cautiously respect as powerful and aloof.
19: Respected Foe	This statue depicts an enemy of the dungeon inhabitants, but one whom they respect due to the honorable nature, combat prowess, or mercy of this foe.
20: Respected Monster	Dungeon inhabitants respect this monster or other great beast, perhaps to the point of deifying the monster or depicting it with powers, faculties, or desires it does not possess.

Memorials (d12)

Dungeons are often ancient locations with long lifetimes, and occasionally their occupants make efforts to record that history. Memorials can be useful ways for characters to learn valuable information about the history of a dungeon and get a particular perspective of events, often from the view of the enemies, the villain, or the original occupants of the dungeon. Roll on this table to generate a particular kind of memorial to feature in your dungeon.

Memorial	Description
1: Burial Memorial	This memorial commemorates the moment of burial or the funeral ceremony of a particular individual or individuals whom the memorial's creators either greatly feared or greatly respected. The scene depicts individuals who respected the individual and may know the secret location of their remains. The memorial may in fact be a tomb, whether this is obvious or not.
2: Coat of Arms	This coat of arms or crest of a particular family or individual contains elements that hint at the nature or past of the family or individual.

Memorial	Description
3: Conquest Memorial	This memorial commemorates a conquest, likely of the dungeon itself or the surrounding region, which took place at some point in the past. It may or may not be from the perspective of the current inhabitants.
4: Cataclysm Memorial	This major cataclysm, likely natural in origin, or at least occurring on an epic geological scale, may have led to the construction or even the creation of the dungeon.
5: Genocide Memorial	Victims of a historical or recent genocide, or those who sympathized with them (or at least sided against their oppressors), fashioned this memorial.
6: Death Memorial	This memorial's creators greatly feared or respected a particular individual or individuals. The memorial may show the scene of the death and give clues as to the true perpetrators. The memorial may in fact be a tomb, whether this is obvious or not.
7: Hero Memorial	This memorial's creators held a great deal of esteem for a particular hero of importance. The current dungeon inhabitants may fear or revere the statue of this hero, depending on their history.
8: Leader Memorial	This memorial's creators held a great deal of esteem for a particular leader or ruler of importance. The current dungeon inhabitants may fear or revere the statue of this leader, depending on their history.
9: Birth Memorial	This memorial commemorates a particularly important birth, which may have taken place near or within the dungeon, of a well-known political figure, holy leader, or supernatural being whom the memorial's creators held in esteem.
10: Rebirth Memorial	This memorial commemorates an awakening or rebirth that may have taken place near or within the dungeon of a religious leader, powerful spellcaster, or even an organization, which was somehow reborn anew from a previous incarnation.
11: Monstrous Memorial	The power and majesty of a particularly mighty beast, monster, or supernatural being is evident in this memorial. The being in question may be understood incompletely by the memorial's creators, but hints suggest its strengths and weaknesses.
12: War Memorial	This scene of a battle, war, or other conflict in which the memorial's creators participated depicts the outcome of the war and atrocities committed, but from a particular point of view.

Dungeon Prison Quirks (d20)

While not all dungeons are actually designed to imprison, many do have a room or apportioned space in which to hold prisoners. The prisons found in these dungeons are often radically different from even the most dangerous prisons in civilized lands. Roll on this table to generate a unique feature to spice up your dungeon's prison.

Quirk	Description
1: Antimagical	This prison is protected with antimagical energy, runes, or specialist security mages. These measures are designed to negate the use of magic by any prisoners, hindering their attempts to escape or cause problems.
2: Arena	This prison is merely a holding cell for combatants awaiting their turn in the arena. The villain or warden forces prisoners to fight each other in regularly scheduled matches, and those who refuse to fight suffer for their defiance. The fights are supposed to be entertaining, so typically gladiators of equal skill level are matched up.
3: Disloyal Guards	Particularly disloyal management, such as the warden or guards (or an equivalent flawed being), can be bribed or tricked with relative ease by would-be rescuers, or prisoners who still have something to offer them after being imprisoned.
4: Enchanting	This prison seems far from unpleasant; it may not even be immediately recognizable as a prison at all. However, it uses positive reinforcement in the form of rewards—such as limitless food and wine or wish fulfillment—to keep prisoners from choosing to leave. There is likely an additional befuddling effect to further trap those who partake in the pleasures of the prison.
5: Experimental Testing	The prisoners here are used as experimental test subjects. Anyone sent into this prison has a limited time before they will be subjected to the experiments of either the villain or the warden. The results might be beneficial or detrimental, or might be guided by the unique goals of the experiment in question.
6: Haunted	This prison is haunted by the spirits of the restless dead, possibly by one specific ghost. This haunting might be a result of the prison's function as a place where prisoners die with unfinished business. Alternatively, the prison was deliberately built in a haunted area, with the ghost providing a useful way to torment prisoners and prevent escape.

Quirk	Description
7: Labor Prison	The prisoners here are used as a source of expendable labor. Likely, the prisoners have access to the area where they work, such as a mine or a workshop, which may even be part of the prison. While the prison guards have been careful to limit access to anything that could be used as a weapon, some of the simple tools the prisoners are allowed to use may be useful in an escape attempt.
8: Magical Observation	Supernatural means allow the villain (or other wardens) of this prison to monitor the prisoners continually and observe their actions and words. Prisoners might be able to manipulate or trick this magic, or else use it to their advantage in an escape attempt.
9: Mind Prison	Prisoners here are either trapped in a state of mental stasis, or else experience a dreamlike illusion (either separate or communally with the other prisoners) created by the villain to keep them comfortable, tortured, or docile.
10: Monstrous Guardian	A beast or monster of legend serves as a guardian. It is likely that few prisoners have gotten (or taken) the chance to face off against the guardian, and a particularly strong or clever prisoner might be able to defeat the monster where others have been too intimidated.
11: Pit	This prison contains its prisoners by virtue of being a sheer, unclimbable pit. Prisoners are likely lowered in, with the intention that they will never leave; there may not even be a path to ascend. Flying characters may be given additional security or measures to restrain them.

Quirk	Description
12: Prisoner Harvest	This prison is not so much a prison as it is a storage area for "pre-corpses." The villain's goal is not to collect prisoners, but to (eventually) harvest their bodies for food, experimentation, or magical uses. While they ideally would be kept alive until the right moment, the villain will likely not hesitate to accelerate the fate of a particularly difficult prisoner.
13: Reeducation Protocol	A villain or prison manager seeks to "redeem" their prisoners, turning them toward a particular point of view for either sincere or malicious reasons. They may have special tools or magic for accomplishing this goal.
14: Supernaturally Guarded	Forces that are more than human guard this prison. Whether they are undead, constructed, or mystical in other ways, they are much more difficult to deceive or elude than equivalent mortal guardians.
15: Torturous	This prison is run by individuals with a penchant for torture, either due to the practical uses of this "craft" or out of a sadistic desire to inflict pain. The prisoners all suffer from excruciating torment and possibly even significant wounds, but a surplus of torture implements and other extreme tools are available as weapons for prisoners.
16: Unbearable Conditions	This prison is intentionally (by nature or manufacture) kept in states of extreme heat, cold, dampness, brightness, sound volume, or other conditions that are particularly unpleasant to the prisoners. This is either to hinder escape attempts or simply to keep the prisoners in a constant state of torture.
17: Utter Darkness	This prison is completely dark; the guards likely don't require light sources, or else bring them into and out of the prison with them. This is by design, to break prisoners and prevent escape.
18: Violent	A culture of brutal violence, likely reinforced by the monstrous guards and/or the villain who maintains the prison, pervades here. The prisoners are particularly aggressive and fearful toward each other and will find it difficult to unite toward a common cause.
19: Webs	Strong strands of webbing or other adhesive material make up this prison. Prisoners are kept mostly immobilized by the webbing, which may be flammable or have other unexpected vulnerabilities.
20: Within the Beast	This prison has been constructed, artificially shaped, or naturally grown within the body of a particularly large monster or beast. It may be that prisoners are devoured and digested, albeit extremely slowly over the course of months or even years. If not, the beast serves as a passive container but will react to escape attempts when it senses them.

Connections (d20)

Any number of passages, tunnels, bridges, and other connections might link the rooms of your dungeon. Roll on this table to generate a connection from a dungeon room that leads onward to the next stage of the adventure.

1: Bridge and Chasm

2: Bridge and Pit

3–13: Hallway/Passage

14–15: Stairs Up

16–17: Stairs Down

18: Vertical Ascent

19: Vertical Descent

20: Vertical Ascent/Descent

Hallways (d20)

Hallways and passages are the most common connections in dungeons, often forming confusing mazes and networks that weave into and around each other. Roll on this table to generate the features of a particular hallway in your dungeon.

1–5: Narrow Hallway (5' wide)

6–13: Normal Hallway (10' wide)

14–17: Wide Hallway (20' wide)

18–20: Extra-Wide Hallway (30' wide)

Stairs (d20)

Stairs are the most common way for adventurers to get deeper into a dungeon. They often serve as the arrow pointing the way forward. Finding the stairs (in or out) might be the main focus of a quest. Roll on this table to generate a particular type of stairs leading up or down in your dungeon.

1: Steep Slope

2–3: Gradual Slope

4–6: Gradual Stairs

7–10: Narrow Stairs (5' wide)

11–14: Average Stairs (10' wide)

15–17: Wide Stairs (15'+ wide)

18–19: Steep Stairs

20: Spiral Stairs

Vertical Connections (d20)

Stairs are not the only way up or down when deep in the depths of a dungeon; other, sometimes more perilous ways to ascend back out or descend deeper into the earth may be available. Roll on this table to generate a unique and interesting vertical connection for your heroes to find in your dungeon.

1: Tiny Chute

2: Small Chute

3: Large Chute

4: Tiny Chimney

5: Small Chimney

6: Large Chimney

7: Simple Mechanical Elevator

8: Basic Mechanical Elevator

9: High-Quality Mechanical Elevator

10: Elaborate Mechanical Elevator

11: Magical Elevator

12: Rickety Wooden Ladder

13: Sturdy Wooden Ladder

14: Chipping Stone Ladder

15: Solid Stone Ladder

16: Rusty Metal Ladder

17: Stable Metal Ladder

18: Stone Rungs in Wall

19: Metal Rungs in Wall

20: Magical Ascent/Descent

Bridges (d20)

Bridges aren't just useful for crossing bodies of water and vast chasms in dungeons; they are also exciting and dangerous locations for conflict to take place. Enemy forces will often utilize a bridge as a particularly useful bottleneck to defend. Roll on this table to see what kind of bridge the party will need to cross to proceed further into the dungeon.

1: Plants/Vines

2: Single Rope

3: Rope Bridge (Fraying)

4: Rope Bridge (Unstable)

5: Rope Bridge (Stable)

6: Rope Bridge (Reinforced)

7: Wooden Planks

8: Wooden Bridge (Rickety)

9: Wooden Bridge (Unstable)

10: Wooden Bridge (Stable)

11: Wooden Bridge (Reinforced)

12: Wooden Drawbridge

13: Stone Bridge (Broken/Crumbling)

14: Stone Bridge (Unstable/Damaged)

15: Stone Bridge (Stable/Solid)

16: Stone Bridge (Reinforced)

17: Stone Drawbridge

18: Zip Line

19: Horizontal Mechanical Lift

20: Magical Bridge (See page 102.)

Bridge Width (d10)

Some bridges are as wide as a road, while others are as narrow as a thread and infinitely more difficult for adventurers to traverse. Roll on this table to generate the width of a particular bridge in your dungeon.

1: Treacherous (This bridge is less than 2' wide)

2-3: Narrow (This bridge is slightly less than 5' wide)

4-5: Thin (This bridge is 5' wide)

6-7: Broad (This bridge is 10' wide)

8-9: Wide (This bridge is 20' wide)

10: Extra-Wide (This bridge is more than 20' wide)

Magical Bridge Properties (d8)

Some bridges display unusual or supernatural properties that make them stand out and possibly make them much more difficult to safely traverse. Roll on this table to see what magical properties might be affecting a bridge in your dungeon.

Property	Description
1: Animated	This bridge appears ordinary, but once characters begin to cross it, it attempts to buck them like a mechanical bull. There may be handholds on the bridge to help keep one's grip, possibly installed by others seeking to avoid being thrown by the bridge.
2: Concealed Bridge	This bridge has been built, modified, or otherwise made to look like the surrounding space through concealing techniques or optical illusions. Care must be taken while crossing it; it is unwise to assume it goes in a straight line.
3: Floating Islands	Irregular floating islands with large or small gaps between them must be jumped or otherwise navigated to cross.
4: Floating Platforms	Floating platforms with large or small gaps between them must be jumped or otherwise navigated to cross.
5: Invisible Bridge	This bridge has been supernaturally enchanted to be invisible to the naked eye. Care must be taken while crossing it; it is unwise to assume it goes in a straight line.
6: Living	This bridge is made out of living material, such as trees, foliage, or even living flesh. It can be wounded or slain like any organic creature, though it may make horrible noises and smells while being attacked. It might even be a cursed being who was not always a bridge.
7: Sentient	This bridge has some semblance of self-awareness, at least when beings are crossing it. It may sound an alarm or otherwise thwart intruders; it may ask them a riddle for its own amusement; or it may be neutral and uninterested in the affairs of mortals.
8: Supernaturally Precarious	This bridge defies the laws of physics and architecture, being too long, too narrow, or too heavy to exist in its current state. It may be extra resilient to attempts to collapse it; otherwise it is especially vulnerable, always on the hair's edge of destabilizing.

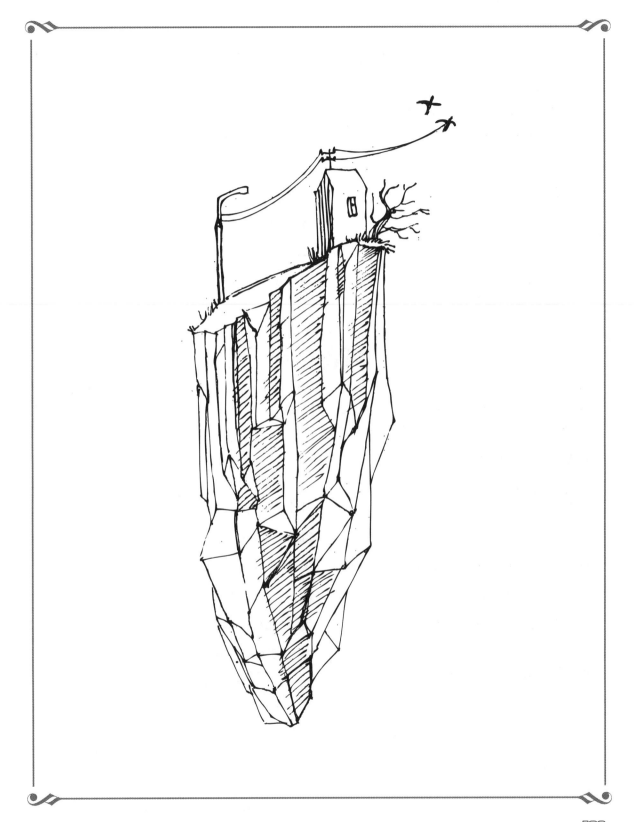

Chasms (d20)

Larger than pits, chasms are often naturally formed by geological shifts in the earth, artificially created by unsafe digging and mining, or induced by a magical cataclysm. Roll on this table to see what kind of chasm the party encounters in your dungeon.

1-4: 50' deep

5-7: 100' deep

8-9: 150' deep

10-11: 200' deep

12-13: 250' deep

14-15: 300' deep

16: 400' deep

17: 500' deep

18: 750' deep

19: 1,000' deep

20: Bottomless

Pits (d20)

Pits are typically artificially created by dungeon inhabitants, often with the purpose of catching and trapping would-be intruders. Roll on this table to see what manner of pit the party (ideally metaphorically) stumbles into.

1-3: 10' deep; rough walls

4-5: 10' deep; smooth, difficult-to-climb walls

6-7: 20' deep; rough walls

8: 20' deep; smooth, difficult-to-climb walls

9-10: 30' deep; rough walls

11: 30' deep; smooth, difficult-to-climb walls

12: 40' deep; rough walls

13: 40' deep; smooth, difficult-to-climb walls

14: 50' deep; rough walls

15: 60' deep; rough walls

16: 70' deep; rough walls

17: 80' deep; rough walls

18: 90' deep; rough walls

19: 100' deep; rough walls

20: Bottomless; rough walls (if any)

Bottom of Pit (d20)

When stuck at the bottom of a pit, an adventurer may find a cold comfort in the knowledge that they are not the first person or thing to fall victim to the pit. Indeed, the bottom of a pit might be riddled with spikes or other dangers, or it might contain a useful tool or clue to help them escape. Roll on this table when a party member finds themselves at the bottom of a pit and wants to keep digging.

1: Stone Spikes (10' long)*

2: Stone Spikes (36" long)*

3: Metal Spikes (36" long)*

4: Metal Spikes (12" long)*

5: Metal Spikes (1" long)*

6: Water

7: Mud

8–9: Muck/Waste

10–11: Jagged Empty Floor

12–14: Rough Empty Floor

15–16: Smooth Empty Floor

17: Dungeon Feature (See page 82.)

18: 1 Body

19: Multiple Bodies (Roll 1d4+1 to determine how many bodies.)

20: Treasure or Oddity

*There is a 25 percent chance the spikes are poisoned.

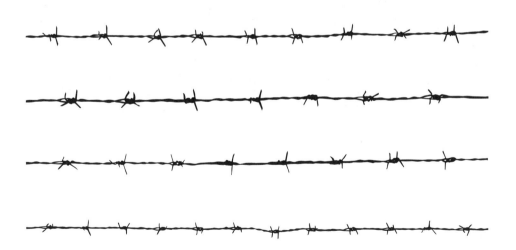

RANDOM TABLES DUNGEONS AND LAIRS

Rivers (d100)

Dungeon environments are often living ecosystems. While some might be built to channel specific liquids through artificial canals, tunnels, and pipes, even dungeons intended to be sealed and dry can spring a leak. When that happens, an unintended river may form that cuts through large portions of the dungeon. Roll on this table to see what manner of river the party encounters in the dungeon.

River	Description
1–3: Lava	This river is made of free-flowing molten rock. It's extremely dangerous to be close to the lava; falling into it is likely a death sentence.
4–6: Acid	This river is made of bubbling acid, which will melt flesh, bones, metal, and many other materials, given enough time. Falling in would be extremely dangerous, not to mention painful.
7: Poisonous Vapors	Heavy poisonous gas vapors flow like liquid through this channel. The poison might boil skin or only cause problems when inhaled.
8–11: Acidic Water	The water in this river has a substantially high acidic content due to chemicals or pollution mixed into the river. Falling in may be dangerous and possibly quite painful.
12–18: Sewage	Garbage, flotsam, and other debris flow in a steady stream. Falling in would be extremely unpleasant and may result in infected wounds or diseases.
19: Oil	Oil, gasoline, or some other flammable substance gives off heady fumes, and anyone who falls in will become soaked in oil until cleansed. If such an individual (or the river itself) comes in contact with open flames, the results will be catastrophic.
20–22: Ice	This river is made from large floes or bergs of ice floating on freezing water, or possibly even a quick-flowing mini-glacier of pure ice steadily moving downstream. Falling in may result in hypothermia, frostbite, or being frozen in perfectly preserved stasis for years.
23–25: Ooze	This thick, viscous ooze may be acidic, poisonous, or otherwise harmful to touch. The ooze may be sentient and possibly able to reach out to attack intruders who stray too close.
26–29: Waste	Bodily excrement, food scraps, bones, refuse, and other waste flows in a steady stream. Falling in would be extremely unpleasant and may result in infected wounds or diseases.

River	Description
30: Blood	This river is made of cold, slowly flowing or hot, quickly flowing blood. The blood likely has a supernatural source, or else has been let from the bodies of sacrificial captives or animals.
31–37: Polluted Water	This ordinary but polluted water contains noticeable quantities of refuse and other substances. Falling in would be unpleasant, and drinking the water will likely result in diseases.
38–60: Dirty Water	This ordinary but dirty water comes from a source inside or outside of the dungeon. It is clean enough to rinse off blood and other substances but may not be advisable to drink.
61–95: Clean Water	This ordinary water likely stems from a fresh source outside of the dungeon. Because of its clean source or quick flow, this water is relatively clean and clear, and likely safe to drink.
96: Souls	Souls of the dead flow in a gray or radiant white ethereal haze downstream. The source of these souls may be a ritual or spell, or a portal to the land of the dead that someone has opened. Falling in could be extremely dangerous.
97–98: Perfume	This river is made of perfume, or more likely perfumed/scented water. It fills the space, and likely the rooms beyond, with a noticeable exotic or pleasant smell and is clean and safe to bathe in.
99: Wine	Wine, beer, or another alcoholic beverage of your choice makes up this river. It may be a result of a large-scale production effort, a delightful magical creation, or a dangerous trap meant to catch the unwary.
100: Liquid Gold	This river is made of liquid gold or some other precious metal, likely superheated past its melting point or enchanted to stay in liquid form. It may be part of a large-scale smithing operation, or a strange and decadent decoration.

Doors & Barriers

Doors (d100)

Though easy to underestimate, doors can be some of the most difficult challenges standing between a party and their goals. Certainly every adventuring party has had the experience of being stuck outside of a door for longer than they or their Game Master ever expected. Roll on this table to generate a door that may present more than just a physical obstacle.

Door	Description
1: Fake Door	This false door is designed to trick intruders into wasting their time and resources trying to open it.
2–5: Broken Door	This door has been at least partly broken down and is relatively easy to bypass.
6–35: Ordinary Door	This door has no locks, traps, or concealments.
36–47: Locked Door	A single lock seals this door. (See page 121.)
48–58: Hidden Door	This door is hidden by a concealment. (See page 118.)
59–71: Trapped Door	A single trap protects this door.
72–74: Fake Trapped Door	Protected by a single trap, this is a false door designed to trick intruders into wasting their time and resources trying to open it.
75–77: Well-Locked Door	This door is sealed by multiple locks (1d4+1 locks in total). (See page 121.)
78–80: Heavily Trapped Door	This door is protected by multiple traps (1d4+1 in total).
81–85: Hidden Locked Door	A concealment hides this door (see page 118), which is sealed by a single lock (see page 121).
86–90: Hidden Trapped Door	A concealment (see page 118) hides this door and a single trap protects it.
91–94: Locked Trapped Door	A single lock (see page 121) seals this door and a single trap protects it.
95–96: Hidden, Locked, Trapped Door	A concealment (see page 118) hides this door, a single lock (see page 121) seals it, and a single trap protects it.

Door	Description
97: Hidden Well-Locked Door	This door is hidden by a concealment (see page 118) and sealed by multiple locks (1d4+1 locks in total) (see page 121).
98: Hidden Heavily Trapped Door	This door is hidden by a concealment (see page 118) and protected by multiple traps (1d4+1 in total).
99: Well-Locked, Heavily Trapped Door	This door is sealed by multiple locks (1d4+1 locks in total) (see page 121) and protected by multiple traps (1d4+1 in total).
100: Hidden, Well-Locked, Heavily Trapped Door	This door is hidden by a concealment (see page 118), sealed by multiple locks (1d4+1 locks in total) (see page 121), and protected by multiple traps (1d4+1 in total).

Door Material (d100)

The nature of doors and barriers in a dungeon can vary depending on the availability of different construction materials and the nature of the dungeon's previous occupants. Roll on this table to generate the building materials for all doors in a particular dungeon or dungeon section, or for one door specifically.

1–4: Dilapidated Wood

5: Cloth

6: Thin Glass

7: High-Quality Cloth

8: Thick/Heavy Cloth

9: Ceramic

10: Chitin

11–13: Rotting Wood

14–16: Wood Logs

17–19: Wooden Portcullis

20–24: Rough Wooden Boards

25–29: Light Wood

30–34: Heavy Wood

35–37: Polished Wood

38–42: Reinforced Wood

43–47: Banded Wood

48: Bones

49–52: Natural Stone

53–57: Rough Stone

58–63: Hewn Stone

64–68: Stone Masonry

69–70: Superior Stone Masonry

71–72: Reinforced Stone Masonry

73: Granite

74: Marble

75: Ivory

76: Thick Glass

77: Rusty Metal

78: Mirror

79: Gold

80: Silver

81: Thick Leaded Glass

82: Brass

83: Lead

84–86: Iron

87–88: Iron Portcullis

89–90: Steel

91: Steel Portcullis

92: Obsidian

93: Thick Tempered Glass

94: Crystal

95: Adamantine

96–100: Supernatural Door (See page 113.)

Supernatural Doors (d100)

Some doors defy the normal laws of reality in their construction or nature. Supernatural doors might guard particularly dangerous or valuable rooms, treasures, or even villains. Roll on this table to generate an interesting and unique supernatural door for your dungeon.

Door	Description
1: Amber	This door is made from a hardened amber or sap-like material. It may be possible to melt through the door with heat, but the viscous sap may not be necessarily easier to move through.
2–10: Animated	Animated by magic and with the ability to move of its own accord, this door can resist attempts to open it. It may be able to fight back or even talk to would-be intruders.
11–13: Animated Bones	This door is made from bones of beasts or humanoids (possibly enemies of the villain) that have been animated to form a barrier and possibly lash out against would-be intruders. It can be opened like an ordinary door or persuaded by those with mastery over the dead.
14–15: Animated Dead Flesh	Made from flesh of beasts or humanoids (possibly enemies of the villain) that have been animated to form a barrier and possibly lash out against would-be intruders, this door can be opened like an ordinary door or persuaded by those with mastery over the dead.
16–17: Animated Living Flesh	This door is made from a solid barrier of flesh that has been animated to form a barrier and possibly lash out against would-be intruders. It can be opened like an ordinary door or persuaded by those who are able to understand its strange nature.
18: Blade Barrier	Made out of whirling blades, this door can slash and cut anyone who attempts to pass through, disable them, or otherwise venture too close. There is a chance someone could time their leap through correctly and suffer minimal damage, but it is a high-risk situation.
19–21: Boulder	This door is simply an ordinary boulder, no more, no less. What makes the door extraordinary is the creature who opens it—a brute of great natural strength or a creature with magically enhanced strength, who is able to move the boulder when ordered to and to leave it in place in the case of intruders.
22–25: Cave-In	This ordinary cave-in may or may not have been caused by magic. The villain and/or dungeon inhabitants have a supernatural means of raising or otherwise getting through the cave-in to the hallways and chambers beyond. Evidence of this method may or may not be present as a clue.

Door	Description
26: Clockwork Construct	This door appears to be a clockwork door of some kind. In actuality it is an elaborate construct that can open and close itself when instructed correctly by its owner. The door is at least as intelligent as a human but rigorously follows the rules and regulations it has been taught to the letter, rather than their intended meanings.
27: Darkness	A sheet of pure darkness covers the doorway. It may impede movement or not, or it may have a worse fate for those who get too close; the darkness must be dispelled or banished by magical light before the way is clear.
28–30: Ethereal Wall	This door is made of another material (roll again on page 111), which has the unique property of extending into the ethereal as well as the material plane. That means that this door blocks the progress of ghosts, spirits, and other ethereal creatures as well as physical ones. This ethereal protection likely extends to the wall it is attached to, as well as other surfaces that would make sense to protect in order to seal off the area effectively.
31–33: Fire	This wall of pure flames does not block passage but must be moved through to proceed. The flames might be mundane, emitting from the walls, floor, or ceiling. The flames might be magical, appearing from thin air and featuring exciting colors.
34–36: Frozen Ice	This door is made of solid ice and must be melted or broken to allow passage if it cannot be opened. The ice might be magically resistant to such strategies or may depend on ambient temperatures to stay frozen.
37–40: Fungal Material	The fungi, such as mushrooms, mold, or even massive spores, that make up this door can be hacked through, but the fungi keep growing back unless the individual spores are burned away.
41–42: Hide of a Mighty Beast	This door is made from the hide of a particularly powerful and thick-skinned creature, such as a giant, a dragon, or a mythical animal. It is precious in its own right as treasure, in addition to being a formidable barrier to bring down.
43: Image	This door is clearly just an image of a door that has been painted, carved, or drawn onto the wall or other dungeon surface. Attempting to open the image will cause it to become a real, actual door, but some precautions may be necessary to avoid further consequences from the door's image.
44: Immovable Air/Wind	A force of unmoving air or wind moves at such high speeds as to block passage. This air must be overcome physically or magically but likely does not block visibility to the area beyond.

Door	Description
45: Interconnected Insects	This network of interconnected insects all respond to the same hive mind. The hive is not intelligent but responds to the image, noises, or pheromones of their master and will part like a curtain in the presence of these signals.
46: Lava	This door either is made of lava that has been magically forced into a door shape or represents a pit of lava that must be circumvented or jumped successfully to bypass the door.
47–48: Liquid Barrier	Some kind of liquid (water, acid, poison, cursed/holy water) is suspended in thin air, forming a barrier that characters would need to wade and push through to reach the other side. This barrier may be thicker and more viscous than ordinary, but it is still permeable for a strong-enough character.
49: Living Creature	A living creature, likely heavily armored, completely blocks the way forward. The creature moves aside for its masters but must be duped in some capacity by intruders wishing to bypass it.
50–52: Magical Crystal	Carved from what appears to be high-quality crystal of some kind, this door has in fact been magically augmented to be as tough as solid steel and will be almost impervious to any but the strongest attempts to batter it down, so long as the enchantment holds.
53–59: Magical Force (Invisible)	Made of a magical force that is invisible to the naked eye, this door appears as an empty doorway. It resists any attempts to open or destroy it. The only way to disable the barrier is through magical means or clever thinking, such as destroying the source of the magic generating the door.
60–67: Magical Force (Visible)	This door is made of a magical force that appears as a glowing door-shaped field of energy and resists any attempts to open or destroy it. The only way to disable the barrier is through magical means or clever thinking such as destroying the source of the magic generating the door.
68–75: Magically Enhanced Stone Masonry	Carved from what appears to be high-quality stone, this door has in fact been magically augmented to be as tough as solid steel and will be almost impervious to any but the strongest attempts to batter it down, so long as the enchantment holds.
76–80: Magically Reinforced Glass	Carved from what appears to be high-quality glass, this door has in fact been magically augmented to be as tough as solid steel and will be almost impervious to any but the strongest attempts to batter it down, so long as the enchantment holds.

Door	Description
81: Magnetic Metal	This door is made from a magically magnetic material that can repel metal to an extreme degree. Characters carrying or wearing metal will have trouble even approaching the door, let alone using metal thieves' tools to open it.
82–87: Plant Material	Foliage and other plants have been shaped to block the way. It can be hacked or burned through, but some magical plants will grow back unless the roots, or the magic, are somehow thwarted.
88: Poisonous Gas	A contained field of poisonous gas does not block passage but must be moved through to proceed. It may seem a simple matter to hold one's breath, but an additional element or trap may thwart such a strategy.
89: Pure Light	This wall of light cannot in any way impede or block the progress of those seeking to pass through it. However, it may come with a trap, trigger an alert, or otherwise have an effect on anyone who attempts to do so.
90–91: Scrying Surface	This door is made from a magical scrying surface—water, glass, mirror, or other—which displays some other famous location or another section of the dungeon (possibly the location just beyond the door) in real time.
92–96: Secret Mimic	This door is actually a kind of shapeshifter disguised as a door, ready to attack anyone foolish enough to seize its "handle" and get stuck to its adhesive pseudopods. The door may wait for the perfect moment to strike, depending on its level of cunning.
97: Shell of a Mighty Beast	Made from the shell of a particularly heavily armored beast, such as a massive insect, turtle, or sea beast, this door is precious in its own right as treasure, in addition to being a formidable barrier to bring down.
98: Smoke	This smoke seems to block progress by slowing down and then repelling characters who attempt to move through it. The smoke can be dispersed with wind or other magical means.
99–100: Waterfall Barrier	This door is made from some kind of liquid (water, acid, poison, cursed/holy water) that flows in a constant downpour to block the way. The sheer force of the liquid may be enough to present an obstacle, knocking characters prone, crushing them, or even eventually drowning them.

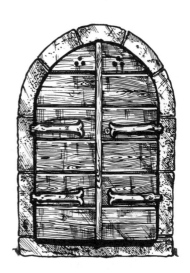

Door Concealments (d20)

Hidden doors are a common sight in most dungeons, and even more commonly adventurers never see them at all. Each door might utilize a different means of concealment to throw would-be intruders off the scent; describing this concealment can be used as a clue to hint at the door's presence or can serve as a red herring to distract and confuse explorers. Roll on this table to generate the nature of the concealment that obscures a particular door or entrance.

Concealment	Description
1: Bookcase	A bookcase slides, pulls, or rotates out of the way to reveal the hidden space beyond. Likely the books themselves serve as part of the key to opening the door, either by manipulating one book in particular or by putting all of the books into a particular arrangement.
2: Carving	A carving in the wall or other surface of the dungeon cunningly conceals the outline of this door and its frame. The carving is likely elaborate and distinctive in other ways to distract observers from the door's presence.
3: Chest	A large chest or cabinet has been placed against a wall or other surface to hide this door. The door is located at the bottom or back of the chest's interior. As large as the chest might be, characters will likely need to stoop or even crawl to go further.
4: False Coffin	This door is hidden in the back of a coffin that is laid against the wall or upon the floor. Multiple coffins with other cargo (or occupants) may be spread throughout the room, making locating the door even more difficult.
5: False Tomb	This door is hidden at the back or bottom of a tomb built into the wall or floor of the dungeon. The tomb may be conspicuously empty or full, to increase the impression that there is no further progress beyond.
6: False Wall	This door is hidden as an ordinary, featureless section of the wall, floor, or ceiling of the dungeon. Characters might easily lose track of this door in large rooms, mazes, and long hallways when there are no obvious features to remind them where it is.
7: Fireplace	A fireplace or similar recess in the wall disguises this door. The back, sides, or part of the chimney of the fireplace will slide or rotate out of the way when properly manipulated. There may currently be a lit fire (magical or mundane) to further dissuade exploration, or as a convenient accident.

Concealment	Description
8: Garbage	This door is currently hidden, whether by intention or by accident, beneath a layer (or behind a substantial pile) of muck, discarded waste, or other such garbage. It may be worth picking through the garbage to find the door, but the smell alone, not to mention the prospect of digging through the garbage, is likely enough to dissuade many an explorer.
9: Hanging Mirror	A hanging mirror hides or conceals this door inside its reflective surface. The mirror might appear to be an ordinary feature of a bedroom or lounge, or it might be conspicuous but magically hard to move.
10: Magical Cloaking	Rendered invisible by magic or another means of cloaking, this door may leave a slight blur or disturbance on the surface as the only visible sign of its presence.
11: Magical Illusion	This door has been hidden behind an illusion of something ordinary and nondescript, such as a section of the wall/floor/ceiling or a room feature (see page 82). Certain magic will detect or pierce this illusion, rendering the door much easier to find.

Concealment	Description
12: Mosaic Tiles	An artistic piece made from colorful ceramic tiles hides this door. Certain tiles or the arrangement of the mosaic may contain clues that might help with finding or opening the door.
13: Overgrown	This door has become overgrown by vines, mold, or other plant or fungal life. An experienced botanist or druid might recognize the unusual pattern of the growth and thereby locate the door.
14: Painting	This door is hidden either behind or magically inside of a painting (see page 87) on the wall, floor, or ceiling of the dungeon. If the door is behind the painting, it must be lifted away, but if it is magically bound within the painting, the characters will need to know the spell or magic to open it.
15: Stairs	This door is hidden either against the wall beneath the stairs (in the "cubby-space") or beneath the steps themselves. The stairs may move, lower, or suddenly change their direction to reveal the secret path.
16: Statue	A statue (see page 89) or some other large or heavy object hides this door. It cannot be detected, or at least cannot be opened, until the statue or object has been moved or lifted out of the way. There are likely grooves, tracks, or other means for assisting in moving the object; that is, assuming the intended opener would require such assistance.
17: Tapestry/Rug	A rug or tapestry hides this door. This may be a large and quite heavy barrier that requires great strength or specific knowledge of the door's location to find effectively. The woven pattern or image may give the necessary clue to locate the door.
18: Wall Mirror	A mirror that either forms part of the wall or has been magically fused to the wall prevents the use of the secret door without the right activation. The mirror itself may open, or a magical door may appear in the mirror to grant passage.
19: Wardrobe	A wardrobe or armoire has been placed against the wall of the dungeon to hide this door. Certain adjustments of clothing or other wardrobe contents might reveal the door.
20: Wine Rack	A dusty old rack, which may or may not still have wine bottles on it, hides this door. The rack does not look movable, but the marks in the dust may tell a different tale.

Locks (d20)

Dungeons are filled with doors, chests, and other places that the party's enemies don't want them getting into. Locks often guard valuables, trap prisoners, or seal away precious areas of the dungeon—in short, everywhere that adventurers want to access. Roll on this table to generate a random level of quality for the lock (or other mechanism) that protects a particular opening.

1: Broken Lock

2: Crude Lock

3–4: Poor Lock

5–6: Mediocre Lock

7–9: Average Lock

10–11: Good Lock

12–13: Superior Lock

14: Complex Lock

15: Magical Lock

16–20: Unique Sealing Method
(See page 122.)

Unique Sealing Method (d100)

Locks are far from the only obstacle that may keep characters from opening a door or other barrier in a dungeon. These unique methods of magical and nonmagical sealing are described in terms of doors, but just as easily could keep shut a chest, armoire, trapdoor, cupboard, or other such opening. Roll on this table to generate a unique way for this aperture to present an obstacle to the characters.

Method	Description
1: Airlock Doors	This set of two doors, one after the other, includes a small hall or room between them. If one door is open, the other seals shut, and vice versa. There may be limited space in the "airlock," so the party might need to split up and move through in smaller groups.
2: Airtight Seal	This door has an airtight fit with its frame, and attempts to pull or lift it open will face not just the weight of the door but the force of the suction keeping it shut. Those stuck on the wrong side of the door may face a limited air supply.
3–10: Barred	A large piece of reinforced wood, stone, or metal bars this door from the other side. Forcing the door open is extremely difficult without supernatural abilities, but if the bar can somehow be removed, the task becomes much easier.
11–14: Blocked by Rubble	This door is partly blocked by rubble, which must be pushed out of the way to free the path of the doorway. The rubble might be on the party's side of the door, making it easy to clear, or it might be pressed against the door from behind, providing an unwelcome surprise.
15–20: Bolted	This door is shut with a metal bolt or bolts that can be retracted from the other side of the door. The bolts fit into sockets in the doorframe and make the door much more difficult to knock down.
21–24: Chained	A chain has been dragged across this door's frame. It is likely bound with its own lock (see page 121). This chain must be removed before the door can be opened.
25: Clockwork Gears	Automatic gears and clockwork mechanisms keep this door sealed tight. The mechanisms are strong but rely upon complex interconnections. Knowledge of its working parts might allow someone to disable the door like a trap or a lock.

Method	Description
26: Code Panel	A complex mechanism with a code panel embedded on it shuts this door. The panel has dials or buttons, possibly bearing runes of numbers or letters in another language, that must be arranged or pushed in a certain order. The combination might be a clue related to the original dungeon occupants or the villain who built the door.
27: Daily Opening	This magically sealed door will only open at a certain hour, such as midnight, sundown, sunrise, or noon. It is likely a short window of opportunity before the door seals again, but each day offers a new chance. It may require exposure to sunlight or moonlight to operate.
28: Disagreeability	Unintelligent and unable to converse, this door does have a grumpy, disagreeable personality and the ability to minorly animate to cause inconveniences and become stuck at the exact wrong moment.
29: Drawn Door	This door isn't immediately visible. Making it appear relies on a combination of a writing utensil (chalk, charcoal, paintbrush, etc.) and a section of the wall, floor, or ceiling, at least one of which must be unique and specific. Using the writing implement to draw an arch or doorway will cause a real door to suddenly appear.
30: Frozen Shut	Ice or some other solidified substance keeps this door frozen shut. This material must be scraped away or melted to free and open the door.
31: Handprint	This door is enchanted to magically respond to a particular handprint, thumbprint, eye scan, or similar unique appendage. Obtaining the appendage, with or without the owner intact and attached, will allow the characters to bypass the door.
32–34: Hasp and Staple	This door is held shut with a hasp and staple, likely with a padlock (see page 121) or pin holding the two together. The hasp and staple are likely on the wrong side of the door.
35–40: Heavy	Particularly heavy, this door must be pushed, pulled, or slid out of the way in order to get around it. This may require multiple strong characters to accomplish and may take more than a few seconds, depending on how strong the characters are.
41: Heavy, with Wheel	This door is particularly heavy and difficult to open but comes with a wall- or floor-mounted wheel. Turning the wheel requires some strength, especially to turn it quickly, but will open or shut the door. The wheel is difficult to destroy and is likely intended to be used by multiple creatures at once.

Method	Description
42–43: Heavy, with Winch	This door is particularly heavy and difficult to open but comes with an attached winch and rope (or chain). Cranking the winch requires some strength, especially to turn it quickly, but will open or shut the door. Destroying the winch makes things more difficult, requiring brute-force strength to push, pull, or slide it open.
44: Heavy, with Windlass	This door is particularly heavy and difficult to open but comes with an attached windlass. Turning the windlass requires some strength, especially to turn it quickly, but will open or shut the door. There is a brake on the windlass to lock the door into a particular position.
45–47: Heavily Barred	This door is barred (most likely from the other side) by a large piece of reinforced wood, stone, or metal. The bar is so heavy, a mechanism or swivel must be operated to raise or lower it. Forcing the door open is extremely difficult without supernatural abilities or siege equipment, but if the bar can somehow be raised, the task becomes much easier.
48: Image Door	This door appears as an ordinary painting, mural, tapestry, or mosaic of a door rather than a real one. The correct activation word, spell, or other trigger will cause the image of the door to become a real one that can be opened.
49: Intelligence	With human-level intelligence or higher, this door has been awakened to carefully assess and spot would-be intruders and will not easily fall for tricks or ruses. It likely knows as much as the villain, or more, about potential invasions of the dungeon and what strategies characters might use.

Method	Description
50: Irised Doors	This door is made from plates of material with sharp edges in the walls, floor, and ceiling. These plates iris open and shut, converging in the center of the doorway. Pushing the plates apart to open the door is possible, but slipping causes the door to iris shut and potentially wound anyone trying to hold it open.
51–58: Loud Opening	This door is sealed or stuck in such a way that it can be opened, but it loudly squeals, squeaks, clangs, or makes some other loud noise as a result. Unless precautions are taken, this may alert nearby dungeon inhabitants.
59–62: Magically Shut	This door is magically sealed shut, and no amount of force will open it (unless the frame of the door itself can be destroyed). Certain magical spells, or the suppression of the door's protective magic, may open the way. Otherwise, a special key or command word is required.
63–67: Magically Stuck	Wedged shut by magical means, this door requires magical abilities or a supernaturally strong push or shove to overcome its inertia. Once the door becomes unstuck, it will likely stay unstuck, but may be hard to shut again.
68: Meltable	This door is sealed by some means (wax, ooze, glue, soft metal) that can be removed by raising the temperature and melting or burning away the seal. It will be difficult to reseal this door in a way that doesn't immediately reveal the absence of the melted material.
69: Monthly Opening	Magically sealed, this door will only open at a certain time of the month, likely corresponding to a moon, a tide, or perhaps a seasonal cycle. It may require exposure to the light of a certain moon to operate.
70: Musical Opening	Magically sealed, this door will only open if a certain song, tune, note, or other noise is created in proximity to it. This may be a melody or hymn dear to the door's creator, or a unique sound or vocal impression that only they could make.
71–72: Nailed Shut	This door has been nailed shut in a hasty and improvised fashion, possibly by dungeon inhabitants forced to flee and barricade the door as best they could. The nails must be pried away, or else the door is significantly harder to open.
73–74: Password	This door is not intelligent or sentient in any way, but it asks any character who approaches for the password, either audibly or telepathically. The password was chosen by the villain or the door's original creator and likely is shared by only the dungeon occupants who regularly use the door.

Method	Description
75: Powered	Strong mechanisms powered from within the dungeon walls by steam, air pressure, heat, water, or some other power source hold this door shut. Thwarting the power source, either by cutting off the door's energy or otherwise counteracting it, will allow the door to be easily opened.
76: Regeneration	This door seems ordinary and appears easy to destroy or break through. However, attempts to break the door down are met with resistance, as the door has a tendency to rapidly regrow its material.
77–78: Reinforced with Spikes	Metal bands stud this door, with spikes embedded in them that protrude outward on either side of the door. Anyone trying to knock the door down will likely end up impaled on the spikes.
79: Riddle	This door is not intelligent or sentient in any way, but it asks any character who approaches it a riddle, either audibly or telepathically. The riddle is likely designed to only allow individuals with certain insight, wisdom, or knowledge but who might not necessarily have been told the answer.
80: Rigged Handle	When gripped incorrectly or carelessly, this door's handle releases (or contains) a trap, harms the appendage gripping the handle, or otherwise hinders attempts to open the door. The door might require extra care to open, or the handle might be avoided entirely.
81: Rune-Protected	This door is magically warded or protected from damage by runes that have been carved into its surface, including the surface facing intruders. The runes themselves might be removed or defaced so as to negate this protection.
82–83: Screwed Shut	This door has been screwed or bolted shut completely from the other side. To open the door, the screws must be released from the other side of the door (a lengthy and difficult process), or they must be destroyed.
84–85: Sealed Shut	This door, and possibly any locks in or attached to it, have been sealed shut with molten metal, which has hardened in place and holds the door shut. The seal must be broken with force or by remelting the seal.
86: Searing Heat	This door is not held shut, but the searing heat that pours forth from it makes it difficult to approach, let alone touch or push open. The characters will need protection from the heat or a way to lower the temperature of the door to proceed.
87: Sentience	This door is sentient but not particularly intelligent or creative, being pre-programmed by the magic that awakened it. It is at least aware of its surroundings and likely will prevent characters from passing unless they can trick the door or overcome the riddle it presents.

Method	Description
88-94: Stuck	This door is badly stuck and requires a solid push or shove from a strong character in order to force it open. Once the door becomes unstuck, it will likely stay unstuck but may be hard to shut again.
95: Toll Door	This door is sealed shut and will open if a coin of the right denomination is inserted into a coin slot on the door. It may require a specific coin, or it may be a coin of surprising or unexpected value designed to fool the unwise.
96-99: Wedged Shut	This door is wedged shut by a spike, wedge, or other simple device that makes forcing the door from one direction more difficult. If the wedge is removed, forcing the door becomes much easier.
100: Yearly Opening	Magically sealed, this door will only open on a certain day of the year, such as a solstice, equinox, or particular date of significance to the door's creator. It may require exposure to the light of the sun on that particular date to operate.

Acknowledgments

Timm would like to thank his family, including his parents, Maura and Ed, for supporting him on every step of his TTRPG-based career, and his siblings, Brendan, Deirdre, and Bridget, for taking the reins on the family D&D game. He also thanks his students and players for allowing him to master his skills with their help and support.

About the Author

Timm Woods is a professional Game Master, educator, and lifelong fan of TTRPGs. He studies TTRPGs as outlets for creative fun and as tools with immense learning potential. He earned his PhD at St. John's University, writing his dissertation on the connections between games and the classroom. He is passionate about working with schools and game-based education in a variety of forms.

Timm runs regular D&D games with students and adults, as well as many other TTRPG. He teaches games and game-based learning through after-school programs and online classes and has worked with numerous New York schools, the US Navy, and companies like Google on game design theory. He has published articles on game-based learning and worked with A24 Film Studios, designing their The Green Knight: A Quest for Honor Starter Set. You can read more about Timm's work at timmwoods.com.